The Elements of Maturity

By

Dr. D.L. Wallace D.Div; PhD

Copyright 2015 by Deliverance Publishing, all rights reserved. All rights reserved. Federal copyright law prohibits unauthorized reproduction by any means and imposes fines up to $25,000 for violation.

Deliverance Publishing, Inc.

Atlanta, Georgia

**ISBN-13: 978-0692539989
(Deliverance Publishing)**

ISBN-10: 0692539980

Table of Contents

Introduction	Page 4
Chapter 1	Page 15
Element one: *The believers understanding that the believer was made for God's purpose and God's glory*	
Chapter 2	Page 60
Element two: *The believer's understanding that the believers life does not belong to him*	
Chapter 3	Page 83
Element three: *The believers understanding that the believer was pre-ordained to do a work for God*	
Chapter 4	Page 120
Element four: *The believers understanding that God has given them gifts and abilities which God intends them to use in His Kingdom and it is the believer's responsibility to discover, cultivate, develop and activate them*	
Chapter 5	Page 169
Element five: *The believers understanding that God intends to cultivate His character in them so that they can become an effective witness for Him*	
Chapter 6	Page 212
Element six: *The believers understanding that his protest of God's activity in his life will prolong God's process and God's process will always proceed the believer's prosperity;*	
Chapter 7	Page 258
Element seven: *The believers understanding that they must learn to move in God's timing and stop expecting God to move in theirs'*	
Chapter 8	Page 304
Element eight: *The believers understanding that their praise and worship is to be based on who God is and not what they experience*	
Chapter 9	Page 341
Element nine: *The believers understanding, that God deserves more than He asks the believer for*	
Conclusion	Page 367

1
INTRODUCTION

Today is an amazing day and this is an amazing time to live in the Kingdom of God. I know someone is saying "he doesn't know me and he doesn't know my story" and you are right, I don't know you and I don't know your story but I know God and I know God's story, and isn't that really the point to know God and to understand God's story? I believe that it is and that until we know God's story we cannot honestly say we know ours. After all aren't we really a reflection of God's will God's story, God's plan? As I look at the world and the events that are happening around us as they unfold I am excited, not at the violence, the conflict and the human tragedy that seems to bombard us from every angle, but rather at how these events are positioning the Church, God's representatives on the earth to be the light on the hill that Jesus spoke of in Matt 5:14-

16 and to provide His wisdom and solutions to society's most urgent problems. Over the last few years there has been a prophetic word echoing through the Body of Christ as if it were the sound of a gun shot bouncing off the hard walls of a hollow cave, moving deeper and deeper into the inner most parts of our understanding, until it has touched the core of our soul and altered our expectations of things to come and our understanding of who and where we are. Prophetic and Apostolic ministries have been born as a response to this new understanding as men and women of God use this sound moving through the Body of Christ as a platform to proclaim their unique and exclusive position in this new move. However, despite all of the attention that has been given to announcing and in some instances debating the existence of the "shift" very little real revelation has come forth about the mature and purpose of the shift. As a result the shift which I am convinced is a

global move of God, has been reduced to another opportunity to focus on our individual needs and the trinkets we desire. But this shift like the shifts that have come before it is about something far greater than our personal needs and desires. It is about the advancement of the kingdom.

I believe that if we are going to understand this shift that is taking place we are going to have to recognize that the word "shift" is simply a term used to describe a movement within the Kingdom of God and as such is one of a number of movements created by God to bring something to our attention to prepare and position us to move deeper into the things of God and further away from the influences of this world. Every shift, and there have been many, is designed by God to highlight, produce or awaken something in us. As I listen to the still and ever present voice of the Lord I hear God challenging us, moving us into maturity. That is the purpose of this book, to challenge those who read it to move into or perhaps I should say move further into maturity.

The question is what is spiritual maturity and how does one know when they have become spiritually mature? For that matter is that even possible? I am sure as it is with any characteristic of the human condition, the answers to these questions are anything but objective and there are opinions as different as the people who hold them. However, maturity is the state of being mature and to be mature is to have attained full growth or development, or having reached a desired stage, especially after processing. So if maturity means to have attained full growth or development, having a desired stage them the question becomes what is the desired stage. I believe that the answer to this question is found in scripture. In both the 8th Chapter of the Book of Romans and the 4th Chapter of the book of Ephesians the Apostle Paul firmly addresses this point. In the 11th through 15th verses of the 4th Chapter of the Book of Ephesians the Apostle Paul speaking of Jesus declared "And He gave some, Apostle; and some Prophets; and some Evangelists; and some Pastors and Teachers; for the perfecting of the saints, for the work of the ministry, for the edifying of the body of Christ: till we all come in the unity of the faith, and of all the knowledge of the Son of God, into a perfect man, unto the measure of the stature of the fullness of Christ: That henceforth be no more children, tossed to and fro, and carried about with every wind of doctrine, by the slight of men, and cunning craftiness whereby they lie wait to deceive; but speaking the truth in love, may grow up into Him in all things, which is the head even Christ." Or as the Amplified translation states "And His gifts were [varied; He Himself appointed and gave men to us] some to be Apostles (special messengers), some prophets (inspired preacher and expounders), some evangelists (preachers of the gospel, traveling missionaries), some pastors (Shepherds of His flock), and teachers. His intention was the perfecting and the full equipping of the saints (His consecrated people), [that they should do] the work of ministering towards building up Christ's Body, (the Church), [that it might develop until we all attain oneness in the faith and in the comprehension of the full and accurate knowledge of the Son of God; that [we might arrive] at really mature manhood-the completeness of personality which is nothing less than the standard height of Christ's own perfection-the measure of the stature of the fullness of Christ, and the completeness found in Him. So then we may no longer be children, tossed [like ships] to and from between chance gusts of teachings, and wavering with every changing wind of doctrine, [the prey of] the cunning and cleverness of unscrupulous men, (gamblers engaged) in every shifting form of trickery in inventing errors to mislead. Rather, let our lives lovingly express truth, in all things-speaking truly, dealing truly, living truly. Enfolded in love, let us grow up in every way and in all things into Him, who is the head, [even] Christ, the messiah, the anointed one." Further, in the 29th verse of the 8th Chapter of the Book of Romans Apostle Paul declared "For whom he did foreknow, he also did predestinate to be conformed to the image of his own son, that he might be the first born among many brethren. "or as the Amplified translations states" For those whom He foreknew-of whom He was aware and loved beforehand-He also destined from the beginning (foreknowing them) to be molded into the image of His son [and share inwardly His likeness], that He might become the first-born among many brethren." Therefore we can conclude from these scriptures that the mark of maturity and thereby the purpose of the shift is to produce the image and likeness of Christ in us. If the Apostle Paul is correct, and I am confident that he is, then how do we know if we are in fact becoming or being shifted into the image of Christ, is there an objective set of standards or guide posts that we can use much the same way we use land marks to assure us that we are going in the right direction. I believe that Christian maturity is not comprised of a single event or thing but rather is a convergence of a number of elements that make up our understanding, acceptance and adherence to the word of God and the basis of our understanding of God, ourselves and the Kingdom of God as a whole.

In this book I will be discussing nine such elements. In writing this book I do not presume that the nine elements of maturity which will be discussed here will comprise the exclusive list or that those discussed in this book are more important than any that others may identify, but rather offer them as what I pray will be a starting point of what will be a life long journey. The elements that we will be discussing in this work as guide post for our journey are:

1) The believers understanding that the believer was made for God's purposes and God's glory;

2) The believers understanding that the believer's life does not belong to him;

3) The believers understanding that the believer was pre-ordained to do a work for God;

4) The believers understanding that God has given them gifts and abilities which God intends them to use in His Kingdom and it is the believer's responsibility to discover, cultivate, develop and activate them;

5) The believers understanding that God intends to cultivate His character in them so that they can become an effective witness for Him;

6) The believers understanding that his protest of God's activity in his life will prolong God's process and God's process will always proceed the believer's prosperity;

7) The believers understanding that they must learn to move in God's timing and stop expecting God to move in theirs'

8) The believers understanding that their praise and worship is to be based on who God is and not what they experience;

9) The believers understanding, that God deserves more than He asks the believer for.

I believe that each of these elements play an important role in the lives of those who desire to live their lives according to the will of God. Further while these elements are interrelated each of them should be addressed individually and will impact the believer's understanding of his/her relationship with God in a separate and distinct way. It is my hope that as we begin our discussion of these elements that you will be both challenged and inspired to examine your understanding of what God requires of you as well as your response to Him. Finally, it is my prayer that this work will challenge you to reaffirm your commit to live the life God has called you to and to experience the joy of living in Christ in a whole new way.

Let's begin!!!!

1

ELEMENT ONE:

The believers understanding that the believer was made for God's purpose and God's glory.

In the world that we live in today and sadly even the Church there is a perception that has gripped us like a snake grips it prey, squeezing us tighter and tighter breaking the spine of true Christian doctrine robbing the Body of Christ of both its definition and its strength. Turning the Body of Christ into a powerless and functionless organism barely alive and waiting to be consumed whole. That perception, that error, that cancer is the belief that "this is my life" and "it is about me". This Biblically inaccurate and narcissistically centered view is destroying that fabric of the Church robbing it of its dignity and validity causing it to implode rather than expand. Further, it has created a leadership vacuum in the world larger than the largest black whole found in space and much like a black whole is sucking both light and energy out of everything it comes in contact with. This perception, this perversion, which has it's roots in a desire to comfort those who are genuinely oppressed and to draw those who are unchurched into the fold, fails at its most basic level to fulfill the mandates of the great commission in that it serves to hinder or perhaps I should say retard the growth or maturity of those who seek to use it as a basic for building a relationship with God much less a life which gives God honor.

In the 7th verse of the 43rd Chapter of the Book of Isaiah the prophet Isaiah speaking on God's behalf declared" Even every one that is called by my name: for I have created him for my glory, I have formed him; yea, I have made him." This scripture raises two points which we would be wise to consider. The first is the source of our identity. Those of us who identify ourselves as Christians have taken on the name of Christ and in so doing signify our intention and our desire to take on His identity. Perhaps the most basic element of Christian doctrine is the doctrine of substitution. It is this principle of substitution that gives power to Christ's submission and to His crucifixion. Without the substitution of identities it would not have been possible for Christ to take our sins upon Him or to die on the cross on our behalf. Further, without the principle of substitution Christ sinless life would not be able to serve as the basis of our justification or righteousness in the sight of God. In short without the principle of substitution our very salvation would not be possible. In addition, even the most basis study of the Bible will make it clear that names convey identity and define destiny. This is particularly important when we consider the name Christian itself. The root of the name Christian is the name Christ which is most accurately interpreted as "the anointed one" this in turn means that a person who identifies themselves as a Christian is by extension identifying themselves as an anointed one, which in fact is our true identity in Christ. Thus being a Christian is more than simply claiming a title it is the setting of an expectation for the benefit of those to whom we introduce ourselves and it is a commitment to represent the one whose name we carry. This is the essence of giving God glory to live a life that demonstrates His nature and likeness to all those who see us, to allow our actions to shed light of the graciousness of God so that all those who look upon us will see a reflection of Him.

The second point I want to make is our origin. In addressing the issue of our origin it is important that you understand that I am not focusing on my or your origin as a singular individual but rather man's origin as a whole. While it is true that God is the source of each of us I believe one of the great errors of the modern Church is we have become excessively individualistic in our thinking and overlook God's treatment of us corporately or perhaps I should say collectively. As a result we often over look clear indications of God's will in search for God will for us in our individual capacity and in so doing pervert God's word in the belief that God's standards and God's instructions apply differently to us individually than they do to the Body of Christ as a whole, all the while ignoring the fact that God is not a respecter of persons and that the 2nd verse of the 5th Chapter of the Book of Genesis teaches us that the name Adam was the name that God gave them, (us corporately) and not him (the one man individually). With that being said, the 26th verse of the first Chapter of the Book of Genesis teaches us that "God said let us make man in our image and after our likeness and in so doing clearly establishes God as the source of our origin.

In examining this scripture there are a couple of things that immediately come to mind. The first is that our creation was intentional. This may seem simple at first but I believe that there is more here than what appears at first blush. God the Father, God the Son and God the Holy Spirit intentionally and thoughtfully entered into an agreement for the creation of man and further determined that man once created would reflect each of them. Thus the creation of man was not an act of evolution nor was man's creation an unintended or consequential result of God creative activities on the earth. The creation of man was a separate and independent act purposely undertaken by God. Man was specifically designed by God to function as God's representative on the earth. Man was created by God for a specific function and purpose, and that purpose was to give God glory.

The second thing I want to point out is the timing of man's creation and man's placement by God was intentional. The 1st Chapter of the Book of Genesis recounts the timing and order in which everything that God made on the earth was made and teaches us that it was not until after everything else on the earth was made that God articulated His desire to made Adam. The 1st through 27th verses of the 1 chapter of the Book of Genesis provides "In the beginning God created the heaven and the earth. And the earth was without form, and void; and darkness was upon the face of the deep. And the Spirit of God moved upon the face of the waters. And God said, Let there be light: and there was light. And God saw the light, that it was good: and God divided the light from the darkness. And God called the light Day, and the darkness he called Night. And the evening and the morning were the first day. And God said, Let there be a firmament in the midst of the waters, and let it divide the waters from the waters. And God made the firmament, and divided the waters which were under the firmament from the waters which were above the firmament: and it was so. And God called the firmament Heaven. And the evening and the morning were the second day. And God said, Let the waters under the heaven be gathered together unto one place, and let the dry land appear: and it was so. And God called the dry land Earth; and the gathering together of the waters called the Seas: and God saw that it was good. And God said, Let the earth bring forth grass, the herb yielding seed, and the fruit tree yielding fruit after its kind, whose seed is in itself, upon the earth: and it was so. And the earth brought forth grass, and herb yielding seed after its kind, and the tree yielding fruit, whose seed was in itself, after its kind: and God saw that it was good .And the evening and the morning were the third day. And God said, Let there be lights in the firmament of the heaven to divide the day from the night; and let them be for signs, and for seasons, and for days, and years: And let them be for lights in the firmament of the heaven to give light upon the earth: and it was so. And God made two great lights; the greater light to rule the day, and the lesser light to rule the night: he made the stars also. And God set them in the firmament of the heaven to give light upon the earth, and to rule over the day and over the night, and to divide the light from the darkness: and God saw that it was good. And the evening and the morning were the fourth day. And God said, Let the waters bring forth abundantly the moving creature that hath life, and fowl that may fly above the earth in the open firmament of heaven. And God created great whales, and every living creature that moveth, which the waters brought forth abundantly, after their kind, and every winged fowl after his kind: and God saw that it was good. And God blessed them, saying, Be fruitful, and multiply, and fill the waters in the seas, and let fowl multiply in the earth. And the evening and the morning were the fifth day. And God said, Let the earth bring forth the living creature after his kind, cattle, and creeping thing, and beast of the earth after his kind: and it was so. And God made the beast of the earth after his kind, and cattle after their kind, and every thing that creepeth upon the earth after his kind: and God saw that it was good. And God said, Let us make man in our image, after our likeness: and let them have dominion over the fish of the sea, and over the fowl of the air, and over the cattle, and over all the earth, and over every creeping thing that creepeth upon the earth. So God created man in his own image, in the image of God created he him; male and female created he them." And we also know that the 8th verse of the 2nd chapter of the Book of Genesis declares "And the Lord planted a garden eastward in Eden; and there he put the man whom he had formed." If we were to examine the source of man's origin, the timing of man's creation and the intentional nature of man's placement on the earth we would see the basis of God's sovereignty over man, which is the basis of God's statement contained in 7th verse of the 43rd Chapter of the Book of Isaiah and it is God's sovereignty over man that is the true focal point of our discussion. God's sovereignty over man, which is God's legal right to exercise authority over man is both innate and relational. It is innate in that it is derived by virtue of God's creative act of both man and everything that man uses, relies on or needs. All of which like man was created for God's purposes and God's purposes alone. Even the grant of dominion to man found in the 26th through 28th verses of the 1st Chapter of the Book of Genesis which provides "And God said, Let us make man in our image, after our likeness: and let them have dominion over the fish of the sea, and over the fowl of the air, and over the cattle, and over all the earth, and over every creeping thing that creepeth upon the earth. So God created man in his own image, in the image of God created he him; male and female created he them. And God blessed them, and God said unto them, be fruitful, and multiply, and replenish the earth, and subdue it and have dominion over the fish of the sea, and over everything that moveth upon the earth" was granted to man for God's glory. How could man who Himself was made in God's image and after God's likeness give God glory without having the right to exercise dominion over the realm in which he lived. It would not be possible for Adam to be in the image and likeness of God, to reflect or shed light on who God is and How God is (which is the essence of God's glory) and not reign over all he surveyed, anything less would serve to diminish the image of God. Equally, God's grant of abundance to man which is found in the 29th verse of the 1st Chapter of the Book of Genesis which provides "And God said, Behold, I have given you every herb bearing seed, which is upon the face of all the earth, and every tree, in the which is the fruit of a tree yielding seed; to you it shall be for meat" Was necessary for man to give God glory. How could man reflect the richness of God and the limitlessness of God's supply, God's sufficiency, or God's generosity if man himself lived in insufficiency and lack. In addition, I think it is important to note that God's grant of abundance to man did not result in man needing to commit a single act of violence or instill fear or dread in any living creature and at no point was the expression of man's abundance the cause of the exploitation of any living creature. But in fact resulted in man giving God glory as man lived in peace and harmony with the creatures man was granted dominion over and as man demonstrated God's compassion, God's goodness, God's mercy as well as God's benevolence towards those that are subject to Him. Further, even God's commands that man subdue and replenish the earth which are contained in the 28th verse of the 1st Chapter of the Book of Genesis are intended for man to give God glory as the earth witnessed the wisdom, order and nature of God expressed through Adam. Even the most basic understanding of the Bible and God's plan for man paints a poignantly clean and painful picture of the consequences of Adam's fall into sin upon all of creation. In point of fact in the 12th verse of the 5th Chapter of the Book of Romans the Apostle Paul speaking on the consequences of Adam's fall provides "Wherefore as by one man sin entered into the world and death by sin; and so death passed upon all men, for all have sinned" and thereby paints a vivid picture of the consequences of Adam's sin. In addition, in the 20th verse of the 8th Chapter of the Book of Romans the Apostle Paul further addressing the consequences of Adam's sin stated "For the creature was made subject to vanity, not willingly but by reason of him who hath subjected the same in hope" or as the amplified translation states " For the creation (nature) was subjected to frailty – to futility, condemned to frustration-not because of some intentional fault on its part, but by the will of him who so subjected it [yet] with the hope" however, despite the incredibly destructive effects of Adam's fall into sin God's plan for man to be an instrument of His glory still remained. As I examine the scriptures it amazes me how consistent God is in positioning man to give Him Glory. Even in one of the darkest periods of human history we see that the assignment, the purpose for which man was created, to give God glory remains. The Bible recounts a period in human history where man had descended so completely into evil that God repented his creation and purposed to destroy them and all of creation. However, in the midst of God's plan to destroy all life on the earth the 8th verse of the 6th Chapter of the Book of Genesis records and amazing statement "But Noah found grace in the eyes of the Lord" and the Bible goes on in the 9th verse of the 6th Chapter of the Book of Genesis that "Noah was a just man and perfect in his generation, and Noah walked with God" In Noah we see a man whose life gave God glory. Through Noah we see God's Justice, God's mercy, God's perfection, God's provision and God's restoration. In point of fact since before the fall of Adam to the coming of Christ into our lives today, man has always been created for God's glory. Through out the history of God's interaction with His servants in the Bible a clear pattern of God using His servants for His Glory emerges as God raises up men and women who would serve Him. One such man was Abram.

In the 1st through 3rd verses of the 12th Chapter of the Book of Genesis the Bible provides " Now the Lord said unto Abram, Get thee out of thy country, and from thy kindred, and from thy father's house unto a land that I will shew thee: and I will make of thee a great nation, and I will bless thee and make thy name great; and thou shalt be a blessing: and I will bless them that bless thee, and curse them that curseth thee: and in thee shall all families of the earth be blessed." Or as the amplified translation states "Now [in haram], the Lord said to Abram, go for yourself[for your own advantage] out a way from your country, from your relatives and your father's house to the land that I will show you. And I will make of you a great nation, and I will bless you [with abundant increase of favor] and make your name famous and distinguished, and you shall be a blessing- dispensing goods to other. And I will bless those who bless you [who confer prosperity or happiness upon you], and curse him who curses or uses insolent language towards you; in you shall all the families and kindred of the earth be blessed- by you they shall bless themselves." In looking at this passage of scripture there a few things that I believe deserve examination.

The first thing was that Abram's obedience to God's command was not optional. It is evident from the language used in both the King James and the Amplified translations that when God spoke to Abram God was not making a request or a suggestion but rather issuing a commandment

"Get thee out". It is truly unfortunate that in the Church of today many have convinced themselves that God's commands are merely life style options, without any regard to the consequences they bring upon themselves as well as the opportunities they miss out on because they choose not to respond to God's commandments with obedience. Think of all the times we have heard God's voice whether internally, through scripture, or perhaps through a third person, directing us to take or refrain from taking a given action, but we choose to do what was right in our own eyes, either because it was convenient or preferable to what God required only to later realize the harm we have caused or the blessing we have missed. When I think about how easily we turn a deaf ear to God's commands to do what seems right to us, I cannot help but think about what the Bible says in the 12th verse of the 14th proverb which reads "

There is a way which seemeth right unto a man, but the end thereof are the ways of death." Just imagine what would have happened if Abram, the great, great grand father of the nation of Israel and the father of our faith had decided to live a life of convenience as oppose to a life that gave God glory. More often than not when God give us a commandment it will require us to do or refrain from doing something that we have not previously imagined was possible and as a result our human nature is to respond with fear and doubt. However in those moments I think it would be helpful to remember that at the time that God commanded Abram to leave everything and everyone he knew Abram hand no previous knowledge of God. In addition, God provided Abram with no training, no support system, (other than Himself) and no clear picture of what the outcome or destiny would be. It is only natural to be overwhelmed by the plan that God has for our lives and face a measure of discomfort at the though of what it will require. Especially since the assignment, whatever it may be is something that you could not possibly do on your own and can only be accomplished through God. But that is really the point that the assignments that God gives us are so far beyond our natural ability that everyone will know that it was really God and not us who performed it, that is how God gets glory.

The next thing that I want to examine is the fact that living a life that gives God glory is not always easy. If we were to examine the commandment God gave Abram in the 1st through 3rd verses of the 12th Chapter of the Book of Genesis we would discover that Abram's act of obedience came at a great personal price and required Abram to take an incredible leap of faith. When the Lord spoke to Abram and commanded Abram to "Get thee out of thy country, and from thy kindred, and from thy father's house, unto a land that I will shew thee" God essentially commanded that Abram walk away from everything he knew, everything that defined him, everything that supported him, everything that comforted him. In order to truly understand the real impact of the Lord's commandment on Abram it is necessary to understand Abram's culture and the role family played in that culture. In today's world families are scattered across different cities, states and even countries and for many family represents little more that a group of people with whom they share common lineage or common DNA. However in the culture in which Abram lived family was everything. In that simple commandment which can be summarized in three little words "get thee out" God commanded Abram to give up everything he valued to show the world that God was all that he really needed, to abandon everything that defined him to become everything God ordained, to exchange what he was for what he would become, but isn't that the ultimate expression of God's glory the transformation from what the world made us to what God ordained us to be. As I think about the choice Abram was required to make and the choices we are called to make, I realize that little has changed, God still calls upon us to give up what we are to become what He intended. When I think of the reality of this choice we face, I cannot help but think of what Jesus taught us in the 44th through 46th verses of the 13th Chapter of the Gospel according to Saint Matthew when He declared "Again, the Kingdom of heaven is like unto treasure hid in a field, the which when a man hath found, he hideth, and for the joy thereof goeth and selleth all that he hath, and buyeth that field. Again, the Kingdom of heaven is like unto a merchant man, seeking goodly pearls: who, when he had found one pearl of great price, went and sold all that he had, and brought it." In these passages of scripture we see something which should shed light on Abram's response to God's command, and for that matter should be impactful to our response to God as well. An examination of the 1st through 3rd verses of the 12th Chapter of the Book of Genesis make it clear that Abram had no contact with God prior to the moment he heard God's command " Get thee out". In the context of the 13th Chapter of the Gospel according to Saint Matthew when Abram hears God's voice for the first time he became the man who finds the goodly treasure (knowledge of God) in the field. I cannot emphasis enough the importance of the fact that Abram had not prior relationship with God. Imagine hearing God's voice for the first time and the first thing you hear God say is abandon everything you know and follow me. What would your reaction be, denial, rebellion, or obedience. Imagine the difficulty and the enormity of that decision. Now imagine the glory God received by the choice Abram made, the importance of God signified by Abram's willingness to walk away from everything for God. I wonder what our choices say about the importance we place on God, how many times we like Abram have been asked to choose between the life we know and the life God ordained, and in those moments what we choose. I wonder how many times we decide it is too difficult to do what will give God glory.

The lesson that living a life that glorifies God is not always easy is taught through out the Bible. Just imagine the years of ridicule Noah endured as he labored to build the Ark in preparation of the flood surrounded by people whose lives mocked God and who had never seen rain, or Daniel who choose to face the fate of being devoured by a lion rather than renounce God, or Meshach, shaddrach and abed-nego who chose to be consumed by fire rather that betray their God and commit idolatry. Each of these men and countless others recognized that it would not be easy to live a life that gives God glory and decided that giving God glory was worth any price. What about you? How much are you willing to pay to live a life that gives God glory?

The next thing we must recognize is that living a life that gives God glory is expensive. As Christians it is a natural expression of our worship experience to focus our attention and our teachings on the gift of salvation freely given to us by our Lord and savior Jesus Christ and to hold fast to the knowledge that we could not and will not be required to pay the debt borne by Him. While this is both a true and an appropriate focus of our worship experience it is but one aspect of our Christian experience and the focus on this aspect alone, or any other single aspect of our

Christian experience at the expense of the rest will result in our understanding of Christianity being imbalanced and immature. Through out the Bible we are taught that living a life that glorifies God is expensive, however it is often hard for us to recognize the price that those who chose to glorify God pay because the price is not paid with money because money is not the currency of the Kingdom. Those who paid the price pay it with humility, sacrifice and surrender, sometimes even to the point of death. In the 5th through 8th verses of the 1st Chapter of the Book of Daniel the Bible speaking of Daniel declares "And the king appointed them a daily provision of the Kings meat, and of the wine which he drank: so nourishing them three years, that at the end thereof they might stand before the King. Now among these were of the Children of Judah, Daniel, Hannah, Michael, and Azariah: unto whom the prince of the eunuchs gave names: for he gave unto Daniel the name

Beltalshazzar, and to Hananiah of Shaddrach; and to Mishael of Meshach; and to Azariah, of Abed-nego. But Daniel purposed in his heart that he would not defile himself with the portion of the Kings meat, nor with the wine which he drank: therefore, he requested of the princes of the eunuchs that he might not defile himself." Just imagine for a moment Daniel, (who was commonly thought to be about 15 at the time of his being transported to Babylon) refusing the kings hospitality in an effort to remain pure in the sight of God. Upon initial examination the refusal of food by a 15 year old boy may not seem like much, (if you have never raised one,) but I want to challenge you to push past the surface and consider it more closely. Daniel, a 15 year old boy, separated from his family, his parents having been forcibly taken captive. In addition to this add the fact that as a prince of Judah he most certainly knew of the unspeakable violence committed by his captures upon those who resisted them. Can you imagine the overwhelming fear that would have saturated the atmosphere and the intense concern for his personal safety, for his fate that he must have experienced, now consider the cultural context in which these events took place. Babylon which is more commonly known by its current name Iraq is and was then in the center of a culture based on pride, honor, shame and revenge. A culture where honor is easily offended and revenge is the natural response to an offense. Add to this the fact that the person whose pride would have been offended and whose honor would have been at stake was the king. At this point I think it should be clear exactly how dangerous of a situation Daniel was in and how risky Daniel's decision to refuse the Kings hospitality and generosity could be. But Daniel was concerned about things more important to him than the possibility of offending a King he was concerned about was honoring a God and remaining usable to Him for His glory. Daniel understood was what was really at stake and that his life required him to chose and chose wisely because if Daniel could not honor both his God and the king then for Daniel the choice was clear. I can hear Jesus in the distant background saying to Daniel what He declared to his disciple in the 10th verse of the 28th Chapter of the Gospel according to Saint Matthew and what I believe He often says to each of us "And fear not them which kill the body, but are not able to kill the soul: but rather fear him which is able to destroy both soul and body in hell". Just take a moment and contemplate the choices that Daniel faced risk offending the King who by all appearances has your natural life in his hands or offend the King of Kings who controls all life in the palm of His. If you were Daniel what would you do, for that matter what do you do when you are faced with this choice? Because each of us faces this choice, do we accept the blessing from the rulers of this world, allow them to define us, become the source of our acceptance, our prosperity, to shape our destiny so we can avoid the risk of their wrath, so we can keep our jobs, our comfort or do we stay true to God. Do we do as Daniel did and reject those things that appear to bless us but actually sever to separate us from God, do we rely on God's mercy to disguise our idolatry and failure to pay the price for what we claim is so important to us. Have we become so conditioned to serve any god that promises to bless us that we no longer think of the real price we pay? Do we even recognize what it means to be defiled, does the concept of being so carnal, so containated, so defiled that God cannot or will not use us? Are we so consumed with being "Blessed" that we cannot see what it costs? I am not suggesting that being blessed is wrong, because the Bible clearly teaches us that God delights in the prosperity of His people. The question I am asking is at what price? Or as Jesus ask in the 36th verse of the 8th Chapter of the Gospel according to Saints Mark "For what shall it profit a man, of he shall gain the whole world, and love his own soul" or as Jesus taught us in the 24th through 33rd verses in the 6th Chapter of the Gospel according to Saint Matthew " No man can serve two masters: for either he will hate the one and love the other, or else he will hold to one, and despise the other. Ye cannot serve God and Mammon. Therefore I say unto you take no thought for your life what ye shall eat, or what ye shall drink; nor yet for your body than raiment? Behold the fouls of the air: For they sow not, neither do they reap, nor gather into barns; yet your heavenly father feedeth them? Are ye not much better than they? Which of you by thanking thought can add one credit unto his stature and why take ye thought for raiment? Consider the lilies of the

Field, how they grow; they toil not, neither do they spin: And yet I say unto you, that even Solomon in all his glory was not arrayed like one of these. Wherefore, if God so clothe the grass of the field, which to day is and to morrow is cast into the oven, shall he not much more is cast into the oven, shall he not much more clothe you, o ye little faith. Therefore, take no thought, saying what shall we eat? Or what shall we drink? Or, Wherewithal shall we be clothed? (For after all these things do the gentles seek:) For your heavenly Father knoweth that ye have need of all these things. But seek ye first the Kingdom of God, and his righteousness; and all these things shall be added unto you." In examining this scripture it becomes clear that we should place our service of God above our desire for the fulfillment of our natural need while at the same time expecting that God will provide for us what we sacrifice for His glory. In the 8th through 14th verses of the 1st

Chapter of the Book of Daniel the Bible provides "But Daniel purposed in his heart he would not defile himself with the portion of the Kings meat, nor with the wine which he drank: therefore he requested of the prince of the eunuchs that he might not defile himself. Now God had brought Daniel into favor and tender love with the prince of the eunuchs said unto prince of the eunuchs said unto Daniel, I fear my lord the King, who hath appointed your meat and your faces worse liking than the Children which are of your sort? Then shall ye make me endanger my head to the King. Then said Daniel to melzar, who the prince of the eunuch had set out over Daniel, Hananiah, Mishael, and Azariah, prove thy servant, I beseech thee, ten days; and let them give us pluse to eat, and water to drink. Then let our countenance be looked upon before thee, and the countenance of the children that eat of the portion of the kings meat: And as thou seest, deal with thy servants. So he consented to them in this matter, and proved them ten days and at the end of ten days their countenance appeared fairer and fatter in flesh than all the children which did eat the portion of the King's meat." In looking at this scripture there a couple of point which warrant mentioning. The first is in order to give God glory we must be willing to do what makes little or no sense when viewed from a natural perspective. Just imagine how foolish it must have appeared to those around Daniel to willingly subject himself to such a meager diet when the kings best was made available or what Abram's friends and family must have thought when Abram walks away from everything he knew to follow a God he had never seen to a place he did not know or how Moses would give up a position of royalty to protect a slave. The second is that living a life that gives God glory requires faith that God has a better way, those who choose a life that gives God glory are not foolish as they are often thought to be, they are those who have faith that God's way is better. Take a look at what Daniel said to the prince of the eunuch in response to his concern regarding Daniel's request "prove thy servants beseech thee ten days; and let them give us pluse to eat, and water to drink then, and the countenance of the Children that eat of the portion of the Kings meat: And as thou seest, deal with thy servant." This statement is not a statement of a martyr planning to die for a cause it is a statement of a man who has faith that God's is his provider, that God's ways are above our ways a man who trust God enough to put God to the test. What about you, how strong is your faith? The next point I want to make is that God only gets Glory if those who submit to His will prosper. As I think about this point the voice of King David speaking the 25th verse of the 37 Division of psalms which says "I have been young, and now am old; yet have

I not seen the righteous forsaken, nor his seed begging bread." Ringing in my ear, David in his years of walking with God, thought the good times and the bad came to what I believe to be one of the most powerfully comforting and life altering revelations we can ever receive, God only gets glory when we prosper. The essence of God's glory is that God nature is revealed when our lives shed light on God's will. In other words the world sees who God is by seeing what happens when we obey His commands. Just imagine what the Prince of the eunuchs would have said if at the end of the ten days if those who choose to eat the King's meat who have faired better than those who choose not to defile themselves for God. Can you hear them mocking God, denying God's power, His wisdom, His concern for those who place their trust in Him. Can you imagine what the enemies would say knowing that Daniel and the other who stood for God having the courage to refuses the command to worship other God's had not been sustained as they stood for God. God can, God knows that it is only our victory that gives Him glory. In the 11th through 22nd verse of the 14th Chapter of the Book of number's there is a discussion between God and Moses which I believe sheds light on this subject which reads " And the Lord said unto Moses, How long will this people provoke me? And how long will they not believe me, For all the signs which I have shewed among them? I will smite them with the pestilence, and disinherit them, and will make of thee a greater nation and mightier than they. And Moses said unto the Lord, then the Egyptians shall hear it, (for thou brought up this people in thy might from among them) and thy will tell it to the inhabitant of this land: For thy have heard that thou Lord art among this people, that thou Lord art seen face to face, and that thy cloud standeth over them, and that thou goest before them, by day time in a pillar of a cloud, and in a pillar of fire by night. Now if thou shall kill all this people as one man, then the nations which have heard the fame of thee will speak, saying Because the Lord was not able to bring this people into the land which he sware unto them, therefore he hath slain them in the wilderness. And now, I beseech thee, let the power of my Lord be great, according as thou hast spoken, saying, the Lord is long suffering, and of great mercy, forgiving iniquity and transgression, and by no means clearing the guilty, visiting the iniquity of the fathers upon the children unto the third and fourth generations. Pardon, I beseech thee, the iniquity of this people according unto the greatness of thy mercy, and as thou hast forgiven this people, from Egypt even until now, and the Lord said I have pardoned according to thy word: But as truly as I live, all the earth shall be filled with the glory of the Lord. Because all those men which have seen my glory, and my miracles, which I did in Egypt and in the wilderness, and have tempted me now these ten times and have not hearkened to may voice." Look at what Moses says to the Lord in verse 15 and 16 "Now if thou shall kill all this people as one man, them the nations which have head the famed of thee will speak saying, because the Lord was not able to bring this people into the land which he sware unto them, therefore, he hath slain them in the wilderness." I think that is both very interesting and very telling that Moses reminded God that if God failed to deliver the nation of Israel into the Promise Land God's enemies who say that He couldn't and that it would diminish God's imagine in their sight and that fact alone was motivation for God not to completely nullify, His promise. Just think if God would be faithful to His promise to those who lived in state of constant rebellion how much more would He do for those who place their faith and trust in Him. I find it interesting how difficult it is for some to live a life that gives God glory especially in light of the number of promises in the Bible intended to give us assurance of the outcome when ever we stand for God. Whether the promise is found in the 1st verse of the 19th chapter of books of Isaiah which provides "if ye be willing and obedient, ye shall eat the good of the land" or the 1st through 14th verse of the 28th Chapter of the Book of Deuteronomy which provides " and it shall come to pass, if thou shalt hearken diligently unto the voice of the Lord thy God, the observe and to do all His Commandments which I command thee this day, that the Lord thy God will set thee on high above all nations of the earth: And these blessings shall come on thee, And overtake thee, if those shalt hearken unto the voice of the Lord thy God, Blessed shalt thou be in the city, and blessed shalt thou be in the field. Blessed shall be the fruit of they body, and the fruit of thy ground, and the fruit of thy cattle, the increase of thy kine, and the flocks of thy sheep. Blessed shall be thy basket and thy store. Blessed shalt thou be when thou goest out. The Lord shall cause thine enemies that rise up against thee to be smitten before thy face: thy shall come out against thee one way, and flee before thee seven ways. The Lord shall command the blessing upon thee in they storehouses, and in all that thou settest thine hand unto; and he shall bless thee in the land which the Lord thy God giveth thee. The Lord shall establish thee a holy people unto himself, as he hath sworn unto thee, if thou shalt keep the commandments of the Lord thy God, and walk in His ways. And all people of the earth shall see that thou art called by the name of the Lord; And they shall be afraid of thee. And the Lord shall be afraid of thee. And the Lord shall keep the commandments of the Lord thy God, make thee plenteous in goods, in the fruit of thy body, and in thy ground, in the land which the Lord sware unto thy Fathers to give thee. The Lord shall open unto the rain unto thy land in his season, and to bless all the work of thine hand: and thou shalt lend unto many nations, and thou shalt not borrow. And the Lord shall make thee the head, and not the tail; and thou shalt be above only, and thou shalt not be beneath; if that thou heathen unto the commandments of the Lord thy God, which I command thee this day, to observe and to do them: And thou shalt not go aside from any of the words which I command thee this day, to the right to serve them." Or the 33rd verse of the 6th Chapter of the Gospel according to Saint Matthew which provides "But seek ye first the Kingdom of God, and His righteousness; and all these things will be added unto you" Or numerous other scriptures which serve to assure those who live to give God glory of God's commitment to honor, protect and provide for them, God makes this point clear.

Yet in still so few in the Body of Christ choose to live for His glory that it becomes clear that faith in God's promises nor faith in God's power are the issue. In fact the issue does not lie with God at all it lies with us and more specifically with our will. I believe the heart of the problem is the lack of understanding or perhaps I should say the lack of acceptance that our lives have never truly been our own and it was never God's intention that we live based on our desires but rather His desire for us. The more closely the Body of Christ in general is examined the more evident how much like Children we really are, and how few of us ever really mature into an adult understanding of our relationship with God. Much like Children what we desire most is to have our way, to live lives fully of pleasure and no responsibility, to have our wants and needs met with out regard to the cost or consequence, to play without regard to the cost or consequence, to play without rules, ready to quit the moment we experience the smallest difficulty. The only problem is that in the Kingdom of God children don't inherit and children do not rule, therefore if we are to received the blessings of Abraham and the dominion promised us through Jesus Christ we are going to have to mature into the spiritual adults we were ordained to be a good place to start in the recognition that our lives were made for His glory.

2

ELEMENT TWO

The believers Understanding that the believer's life does not belong to Him.

As I begin this Chapter I find myself reflecting on the number of members of the Body of Christ who began this day, as they have countless days before it, laying before God petitioning God seeking God's assistance to accomplish the goals they have set for themselves. Goals that are based on the priorities they have established for themselves based on the image they hold of how their life should be and the desires they want or need fulfilled. Most of the Body of Christ knowingly or unknowingly based their petitions and more often than not their expectations of what they will be granted by God on the underlying belief that they have a fundamental right to lead their life as they determine best and based that belief on the commonly held assumption that their life belongs to them and consequently they have the right to control it. This belief is rooted in the subconscious belief in personal sovereignty, that they more than anyone else have the right to control and use their lives, time, talents and gifts, therefore they should be used to serve them. The only question is what if God does not agree? More to the point, what if God who is truly sovereign believes that His right to use our lives, our time, our talents and our gifts should and does in fact supersedes ours. What if God believes that our lives are in fact not ours, but His? Further what if God considers our attempt to live our lives for ourselves and not for Him to be unreasonable?

In the 5th verse of the 1st chapter of the Book of Jeremiah the Bible declares something that I believe is worthy of our consideration when God said " Before I formed thee in the belly I knew thee; and before thou camest forth out of the womb I sanctified thee, and ordained thee a prophet unto the nations" or as the Amplified translation provides " Before I formed you in the womb I knew and approved of you [as my chosen instrument], and before you were born I separated and set you apart, consecrating you, and I appointed you a prophet to the nations" As I consider the implications of this statement I find it interesting that both we and God both assert a legal right of ownership to out lives. Further since both we and God assert such claims of ownership which in most cases cannot be reconciled, the question becomes which claim is greater our claim which can only be based on our existence or God's claim which is based on our creation. As I examined the issue of legal ownership there was one fact that became clear immediately, God's claim of ownership is first in time. In the 5th verse of the 1st Chapter of the Book of Jeremiah

God declared "before I formed in the womb I knew thee" Isn't that amazing that God's right to ownership of each of us predates our conception, that God not only knew us but planned and purposed our lives before we were conceived. Our right to ownership could not possibly predated God's because God's right to ownership originates prior to our knowledge of ourselves.

Another point that becomes immediately clear is that God's right to ownership is first in right. In the 1st and 2nd verses of the 1st chapter of the Book of Genesis we see that God's position of first in right is based on three distinct facts. The first is found in the 26th and 27th verses of the 1st Chapter of the Book of Genesis when God declared "And God said, let us make man in our image, after our own likeness: and let him have dominion over the fish of the sea, and over the fowl of the air, and over the cattle, and over all the earth, and over every creeping thing that creepth upon the earth. So God created man in his own image. In the image of God he created he him; male and female he created them." In these passages of scripture we see that God is not only the creator of man but the conceiver of man, that man was conceived in the mind of and heart of God and as such God is the source of man's origin. Much the same way an inventor or an artist has the right to what they create through the fruit of their intellect or imagination, God as the creator of man has the right of ownership of man by virtue of His act of creation. The second basis for God's position as first in right is found in the 7th verse of the 2nd chapter of the Book of Genesis which declares "And the Lord God formed man of the dust of the ground". In this scriptural passage the Bible teaches us that man was not only created by God, but was also constructed from material, (dust) made and owned by God. If God is the creator of the earth as the 1st Chapter of the

Book of Genesis declares that He is, then it stands to reason that God is the owner of the earth He created and if God owns the dust which He used to form man then if follows that God would still own the dust once it was in the form of man. The third and final basis for God's position as first in right is found in the second part of the 7th verse of the 2nd Chapter of the Book of Genesis which provides "and breathed into his nostrils the breath of life and man became a living soul" In this scripture the Bible makes it clear that it was God's intentional action of breathing His breath into man that resulted in man having life. Each of these things establishes that God's right to ownership predates our birth and our lives literally belong to God. But perhaps the most important basis for God's ownership stems from our redemption. So then the question becomes what does the Bible mean by redemption? Redemption or to be redeemed is to be ransomed in much the same way a price would be paid to a kidnaper for the return of a child, God paid a price for our return. However the price was not paid in money, it was paid in the shed blood of Jesus. Interestingly enough the very act of redemption in and of itself at validates God's position of owner of man because by definition you cannot ransom what does not belong to you. In the 19th and 20th verses of the 6th Chapter of the 1st Book of Corinthians the Apostle Paul spoke directly on the subject of God's right of ownership through the act of redemption when he declared "know ye not that your body is the temple of the Holy Ghost which is in you, which ye have of God, and ye are not your own? For ye are brought with a price" therefore glorify God in your body, and in your spirit, which are God's" or as the Amplified translation states " Do you not know that your body is the temple-the very sanctuary- of the Holy Spirit who lives within you, whom you have received [as a gift] from God? You are not your own, you were brought for a price-purchased with a preciousness and paid for, made His own. So then honor God and bring glory to Him in your body." In addition in the 23rd verse of the 7th Chapter of the 1st Book of Corinthians the Apostle Paul declared " ye are brought with a price; be not ye servants of men" or as the Amplified translation states " you were brought with a price-purchased with a preciousness and paid for[by Christ]; then do not yield yourselves up to become{in your own estimations} slaves to men; {but consider yourselves slaves to Christ}" what amazes me most about these scriptures is not only the truth they reveal about the proper condition of our lives in Christ, that we are the temples, the dwelling places of the Holy Spirit, which is an incredible honor, but how gentle and unassuming God actually is in asserting His right of ownership. It is unfortunate that there are so many people in the world and in the Church who see God as harsh, unreasonable and even cruel, a God who denies man the right to enjoy his life and forces man into a life of unbearable service in exchange for the hope of salvation and the avoidance of eternal damnation. As a result they seek to stay as far away from God as possible and only seek God either out of a sense of duty or a state of desperation. What is even more unfortunate is that there are those in ministry that God has called to glorify him and desires to advance the gospel through who perpetuate this image. However, this characterization of God is simply untrue. In fact scripture plainly teaches us that God does not force us to surrender our lives to Him even though He has both the power and the right to do so. In the 1st and 2nd verses of the 12th Chapter of the Book of Romans the Apostle Paul gives us a clear example of God's methods of getting people to surrender the life that He owns to Him when he declared" I beseech you therefore, brethren, by the mercies of God, that ye present your bodies a living sacrifice, Holy, acceptable to God, which is your reasonable service. And be not conformed to this world but be ye transformed by the renewing of your mind, that ye may prove what is the good, acceptable and perfect will of God." Or as the Amplified translation states " I appeal to you therefore, brethren, and beg of you in view of [all] the mercies of God, to make a decisive dedication of your bodies-presenting all your members and faculties-as a living sacrifice, holy (devoted, consecrated) and well pleasing to God, which is your reasonable (rational, intelligent) service and spiritual worship. Do not be conformed to this world-this age, fashioned after and adopted to its external, superficial customs. But be transformed (changed) by the [entire] renewal of your mind-by its new ideals and its new attitude-so that you may prove {for yourself} what is the good and acceptable and perfect will {in His sight} for you." In looking at this scripture there are a number of points that warrant examining. The first is the means God uses to effect our surrender. In this scripture the Apostle Paul begin his discussion in an interesting manner "I appeal to you" or "I beseech you" it is evident from the language used here as well as the comments which follow that God is not using the Apostle to issue a command but rather an appeal. I think that it warrants repeating that the Apostle Paul is not issuing a demand that we present our bodies but rather is making an appeal that we do so, I find it interesting that the creator of the universe, the sovereign God, the all powerful God, who destroyed the World in a flood is not attempting to compel our compliance but is instead appealing to us for our cooperation. As I reflect on this point I am overwhelmed by the gentleness with which God deals with us, much like a father who patiently teaches his children to do what is best for them. Contrast this picture of God's true nature with the image of a wrathful impatient God that is often projected in secular society and even portions of the Church. God who is all powerful could most certainly compel us to surrender our lives to Him and would be well within His legal and moral right (authority) to do so, but He instead chose not to force but to persuade us. The second point I want to examine is that God desires our surrender to be based on our knowledge of His nature and His activities in our lives. In the 1st verse of the 12th chapter of the Book of Romans the Apostle Paul wrote "I appeal to you therefore, brethren, and beg of you in view of [all] the mercies of God" (Amp). In other words the Apostle Paul is basing his request upon their (our) knowledge of God's goodness, and not fear of God's wrath. When I think about the Apostle Paul's appeal I cannot help but think about the amazing history of the Nation of Israel, and all of the points where their History was intersected and impacted by the mercy of God, from the birth of Isaac to the favor God showed Jacob when he was living with Laban, to God's use of Joseph to provide for the Nation of Israel during the years of famine, to the favor they found while living in Egypt, to God's deliverance of them from Egyptian bondage, to God's parting of the red sea, to the hundreds if not thousands of occasions where the Nation of Israel experienced God's supernatural power working on their behalf and I cannot help but ask myself hasn't God done enough to earn their trust? Hasn't God done enough to earn ours? You may not have had these experiences but I am sure you have had your own. When was the last time you devoted some time to rehearsing the story of what God has done for you in your mind? Isn't your story filled with enough instances of

God's mercy for you to have come to trust Him? I cannot emphasis this point enough that God expects that the instances of His mercy will become the basis of our trust and our trust to be the basis of our surrender. But isn't this the real test of maturity, the ability or perhaps I should say the willingness to recognize the patterns in our lives and base our belief and our responses upon those patterns. Does the history of God's activity in your life establish the fact that God is worthy of your trust and your surrender. The next point I want to make is that God intends our surrender to be voluntary. When I think about what the Apostle Paul wrote in the 1st verse of the 12th Chapter of the Book of Romans when he admonished us by saying "make a decisive dedication of your bodies-presenting all your members and faculties- as a living sacrifice" I think about a bride walking down the isle on her wedding day. How intentional she is as she walks down the isle to present herself to her future husband, the extreme care that was taken in the selection of her dress and every item of clothing and piece of jewelry. The joy she feels as she contemplates how much fuller, more joyful, happier her life will be joined to her husband than it was before. I imagine her thinking about all the special moments she has shared with him, all the expressions of his love she has experienced. This image is what I believe the Apostle Paul meant when he spoke of making a decisive dedication of your bodies. In addition I believe our making such a dedication is the fulfillment of the promise we made when we made a public confession of Jesus Christ as our Lord when we received the gift of salvation. The question is how long should your groom, (Jesus Christ) have to wait? Can you imagine a wedding where the bride refused to walk down the isle or did so reluctantly? What would that say to the groom who has spent months if not years preparing for life with his bride, providing her with food, shelter, love, security, investing his time and energy in her to demonstrate his love and devotion to her, his trustworthiness, only to see or hear her acknowledge all that he has done for her while she still refuses to walk down the isle, would you consider her actions to be reasonable? More importantly, what do you think God would say? This question brings me to my next point, God sees out failure to surrender our lives to Him as unreasonable.

In the 1st verse of the 12th Chapter of the Book of Romans the Apostle Paul Admonished us "to make a decisive dedication of your bodies-presenting all your members and faculties-as a living sacrifice, holy (devoted, consecrated) and well pleasing to God, which is your reasonable (rational intelligent) service and spiritual worship" as I read this passage of Scripture I became acutely aware of how different our point of view is from God's. What we often think is a cause of celebration is merely reasonable in the sight of God and what we think of as a "reasonable" normal relationship with God is often viewed as unreasonable and ill-rational in His sight. This fact reminds me of what Jesus taught us in the 15th verse of the 16th Chapter of the Gospel according to Saint Luke which provides "Ye are they which justify yourselves before men; but God knoweth your hearts: for that which is highly esteemed among men is abomination in the sight of God". As I think about this statement I imagine about how we who are members of the body of Christ often lead our lives and how little our lives, (not our profession of our faith and commitment) really differ from those who do not believe. How many of us truly live a life focused on serving God, not being blessed by God, serving Him. How much of God's will do we do when it is not convenient, when it might cost us friendships, a job, a relationship with a family member, when it may place our comfort or our economic stability at risk? How many of us really show up when it really and truly matters? What if the reason we are struggling to win the lost to Christ is because when they look at their lives, their motivations, their commitment to God and ours they cannot see a difference? If we are honest, how many of us can truly say we have surrendered our lives to God so He can do with them whatever pleases Him. For those who cannot, how much thought have you given to how God views your failure to do so. If the Apostle Paul is correct God views our failure to surrender to Him as unreasonable. One of the major reasons for what I can only describe as spiritual disconnection is the difference between the underlying assumptions upon which many of us have built our lives and God's actually intentions. In the world in which we live, man and the desires of man are the focal point of everything, everything we hear, see, smell, touch, taste, or experience, including the seemingly never ending conflict and violence that surrounds us is an intended or unintended consequence of man's desires. As a result it is only natural for us to believe that God shares our focus. However the fact of the matter is God does not!!! God's focus is His will and His desires not ours and given as the Bible declared in the 8th verse of the 55th Chapter of the Book of Isaiah " my thought are not your thoughts, neither are my ways your ways, saith the Lord For as the heavens are higher than the earth, so are my ways higher than your ways, my thought than your thoughts" we should not expect that God would change His focus to become ours, but rather change ours until they to become His. We should always expect God to do what is right in His sight and not what is right in ours. The Apostle Paul addressed this point in the 2nd verse of the

12th Chapter of the Book of Romans when he instructed us "And be not conformed to this world: but be ye transformed by the renewing of your mind, that ye may prove what is that good, and acceptable, and perfect will of God" or as the amplified translation states "Do not conform to this world-this age, fashioned after and adapted to its external, superficial customs. But be transformed (changed) by the [entire] renewing of your mind-by its new ideals and its new attitudes-so that you may prove [for yourselves] what is the good and acceptable and perfect will of God, even the thing which is good and acceptable and perfect [in His sight] for you." In examining this scripture it becomes evident that the purpose of the surrender God requires is the transformation that God desires. It should be equally evident that the reason we are so unwilling to surrender is that we have conformed to this world, our values, our ideals, our definitions of success, our desires, our concept of happiness are all derived from a world that we are called to be separate from. Imagine how much easier it would be to surrender to God if all of your expectations, desires, ideals and concepts of happiness came from Him. If we loved what He loved and hated what He hated, if we identified with Him and not them. Imagine how easy it would be if we understood our lives and our purposes from God's point of view. Just think how much easier your walk with God would be if your understanding of life lined up with what the Apostle Paul taught us in the 28th and 29th verses of the 8th Chapter of the Book of Romans when he declared "and we know that all things work together for good to them that love God, to them who are the called according to His purpose. For whom he did foreknow, he also did predestinate to be conformed to the image of his son, that he might be the first born among many brethren." How much easier it would be to present your body to God as a living sacrifice if all you wanted was God's will. But our will or at least our stubborn commitment to the fulfillment of it is first and foremost a lack of spiritual maturity, a failure to grasp and perhaps to even consider what I believe to is one of the most fundamental principles of Christianity which is that it is not about us, we are not the central figure around which things revolve Jesus is. As I raise this point I am reminded of a statement made by the Apostle Paul in the 14th and 15th verses of the 5th Chapter of the 2nd Book of Corinthians when he declared "For the love of Christ constrains us; because we thus judge, that if one died for all then were all dead: and that he died for all, that they which live should not henceforth live unto themselves, but unto him which died for them, and rose again." Or as it is expressed in the amplified translation "for the love of Christ controls and urges and impels us, because we are of the opinion and conviction that [if] one died for all, then all died; and He died for all, so that all those who live might live no longer to and for themselves, but to and for him who died and was raised again for their sakes." It is evident that it was God's intent that those who Christ died for should live for Christ and not for themselves. The question is who do you truly live for, to say you live for Christ is one thing but to live for Christ is another. So the real question is what do your decisions say to those who are watching you, what do they learn about your spiritual maturity by the life your live and the actions you take.

3.

ELEMEMT THREE

The believers understanding that the believer was preordained to do a work for God.

In contemporary society it is commonly believed that each of us are independent beings who are free to define ourselves and who posses the right to shape and determine our lives as we see fit. That our lives belong to us and we are the master of our own fate, Along with this belief comes the understanding that each of us are responsible for and to ourselves and are only accountable to those people and for those things we agree to. This view which is quite common in the world and even certain segments of the Church recognizes no higher order or purpose and makes each of us the center of our own world and our personal goals and ambitions the focal point of our lives and the determining factor of our success. But what if those who hold this world view, those who have made the goal of personal fulfillment their primary, if not singular objective are wrong? What if the right to define ourselves, to chart our own course for our lives really does not exist? What if you and I were made for reasons far larger than ourselves, what if you were born for a purpose, if there was more to your life, my life, than personal success? I believe this question is one of the most profound questions in the world in which we live. The question of why I am here or what is my purpose goes to the core of how we perceive and understand everything around us including our understanding of God and His role in our lives.

For those who believe that they are here to fulfill their personal desires and ambitions, God is their provider and their interaction with God is from the vantage point of God as a source. However, for those who see their purpose from a much broader and perhaps more comprehensive perspective their understanding of God is broader as well. However the truth of the matter is regardless of what our particular view on the subject may be the answer to the question why I am here is of paramount importance to each of us, and more significantly perhaps, it is important to God. It is important to God not simply because it is important to us but rather because how we answer this question will determine how are relationship with God will develop and how much or how little of God we will receive and for that matter how much of God we will desire.

The truth of the matter is that we are most likely to receive what God has to say when we agree with what He is saying and are most likely to reject what God is saying when what God says is in opposition to what we think, feel or desire. When I think of how our preconceived notions determine how much of what we will receive from God I am reminded of the statement made by Jesus in the 13th through 15th verses of the 13th Chapter of the Gospel according to Saint Matthew which declares "Therefore speak I to them in parables: because they seeing see not; and hearing they hear not, neither do they understand. And in them is fulfilled the prophecy of Esaias, which saith, By hearing ye shall hear and not understand; and seeing ye shall see and shall not perceive: For this people's heart is waxed gross, and their ears are dull of hearing and their eyes they have closed; lest at any time they should see with their eyes, and hear with their ears, and should understand with their heart, and should be converted, and I should heal them." Or as the amplified Translation states " This is the reason that I speak to them in parables, because having the power of seeing they do not see, and having the power of hearing they do not hear, nor do they grasp and understand. In them indeed is the process of fulfillment of the prophecy of Isaiah which says: you shall indeed hear and hear, but never grasp and understand; and you shall indeed look and look, but never see and perceive. For this nation's heart has grown gross-fat and dull; and their ears heavy and difficult of hearing, and their eyes they have tightly closed, lest they see and perceive with their eyes, and hear and comprehend the sense with their ears, and grasp and understand with their heart, and turn and I should heal them." In this scripture Jesus makes it clear it is our hardheartedness and our willfulness that causes us to not truly hear what God is saying to us. Therefore in light of this revelation the question we should be asking ourselves is what did God say about why we are here and did we hear Him when He said it and if we did not hear

Him, why? Through out the Bible, even as early as the story of our creation, God makes it abundantly clear that we were created for the purpose of carrying out God's will and not ours. In the 26th through 28th verses of the 1st Chapter of the Book of Genesis the Bible speaking about God's intention to create man states "And God said, let us make man in our image, after our likeness: and let them have dominion over the fish of the sea, and over the fowl of the air, and over the cattle, and over all the earth, and over every creeping thing that creepth upon the earth. So God created man in His image, in the image of God created He him male and female created He them. And God blessed them, and said unto them, Be fruitful and multiply, and replenish the earth, and subdue it: and have dominion over the fish of the sea, over the fowl of the air, and over every living things that moveth upon the earth" thereby establishing the fact that man was created by God to perform a specific work on the earth. I find it interesting that God assigned man a work before man was created. A fact which is supported through out the Bible and strengthens the proposition that man was created to do a work for God in as much as the need for the work to be performed existed prior to the creation of the man created to perform it. If we were to examine these passages of scripture it would become evident that man's creation, his grant dominion, as well as his grant of provision were established not for man but for the purpose of giving man the ability to perform the work for which He was preordained by God. This point is made abundantly clear by the words God Himself spoke to the prophet Jeremiah in the 5th through 10th verses of the 1st Chapter of the Book of Jeremiah which provides" Before I formed thee in the belly I knew thee; and before thou camest forth out of the womb I sanctified thee, and I ordained thee a prophet unto the nations, Then said I, oh Lord God: behold, I cannot speak: for I am a child. But the Lord said unto me, say not, I am a child: for thou shalt go to all that I shall send thee, and what so ever I command thee thou shalt speak. Be not afraid of their faces: for I am with thee to deliver thee saith the Lord, then the Lord put forth his hand, and touched my mouth, and the Lord said unto me, behold, I have put my words in thy mouth. See I have this day set thee over the nations and over kingdoms, to root out, and to pull down, and to destroy, and to throw down, to build, and to plant." Or as the Amplified translation states "Before I formed you in the womb I knew and approved of you [as my chosen instrument] and before you were born I separated and set apart, consecrating you, and I appointed you a prophet to the nations. Then said I, oh Lord God: Behold, I cannot speak, for I am only a youth. But the Lord said to me, say not, I am only a youth; for you shall go to all to whom I shall send you, and whatever I command you shall speak, Be not afraid of them[their faces], for I am with you to deliver you, says the Lord. Then the Lord put forth His hand and touched my mouth. And the Lord said to me, Behold, I have put my words in your mouth, See I have this day appointed you the oversight of the nations and of the kingdoms, to root out and pull down, to destroy and to overthrow, to build and to plant." In examining these passages of scripture there are a few points that I believe that are vital to our discussion.

The first point that I believe that is vital to our understanding is that we were created to do God's work. In the 29th and 30th verses of the 8th Chapter of the Book of Romans the Apostle Paul declared "For whom he did foreknow, he also did predestine to be conformed to the image of His son, that He might be the first born among many brethren. Moreover, whom He did predestine, them

He also called: and whom He called, them He also justified: and whom He justified, them He also glorified" In this scripture it becomes clear that God pre-ordained us to serve Him. Many of us in the Church speak of being called to preach or called to worship or called to serve in some capacity and point to that call as the point that God made a decision that we are to sever Him and in so doing miss the larger truth. Further our failing to recognize that God's choice predates the "call" leads us into the error of believing that we have the right to chose whether or not we will comply and what is worse that if we fail to comply God will simply call or select someone else. In this sense we reduce ourselves down to something far less than what we truly are. As we persist in this error we focus on what is most common about us, our age, our appearance, our career and our short comings and as a result overlook the unique greatness that has been placed inside each of us. I firmly believe that the reason behind this gross and tragic error is our failure to both see God in us and to see God's hand in our personal history and circumstances and as a result never come to recognize the pattern of our spiritual finger print, that thing that distinguishes us from everyone else. But just imagine for a moment if you truly are unique and every event in your life from the choice of the genetic make up of your parents, you height, natural weight, mental processes, experiences, intellectual bent, friendships even the struggles you faced were designed by God to shape you into a specific person to fulfill a specific work for God. What if you were called to do it but rather than obey and complete it, whatever your particular it may be you decide to fulfill your will instead. Some might ask, if I was made for it, then what about the "call", what purpose does the call that the Bible refers to in the 29th and 30th verses of the 8th Chapter of the Book of Romans serve.

The simple answer is that it serves as an announcement. If we were to examine the declaration of the Lord to the young prophet Jeremiah found in the 5th through 10th verses of the 1st Chapter of the Book of Jeremiah which declares "Before I formed thee in the belly I knew thee; and before thou camest forth out of the womb I sanctified thee, and I ordained thee a prophet unto the nations. Then said I, Oh, Lord God: behold, I cannot speak: for I am a child. But the Lord said unto me, say not, I am a child: for thou shalt go to all that I shall send thee, and whatsoever I command thee thou shalt speak. Be not afraid of their faces: for I am with thee to deliver thee, saith the Lord. Then the Lord put forth His hand, and touched my mouth. And the Lord said unto me, Behold, I have put my words in thy mouth. See, I have this day set thee over the Nations and over Kingdoms, to root out, and to pull down, to build, and to destroy." There a few things that would become evident. The first is that when the Lord spoke to the prophet Jeremiah in the 5th verse God was speaking in the past and not the present tense. The "Lord said I knew thee" and "I sanctified thee" and "I ordained thee" not I know thee, I am sanctifying thee or I am ordaining thee. This is important because it establishes that the purpose of this declaration was to inform Jeremiah of what God had already done not what God was doing or was about to do. The second point is that these verses of scripture serve as an announcement of Jeremiah's identity. It is clear from the 5th verse that prior to God speaking to Jeremiah in this discourse that Jeremiah did not know who he was or that he was ordained to be a prophet and was unaware of God's plan and purpose for his life. Further, like us, Jeremiah would have no way of coming into a true understanding of who he was or what he was ordained to do unless and until he heard God's voice. I think it is safe to assume that

Jeremiah was leading his life based on his understanding or the understanding of those who influenced his decision making process as well as his sense of what was right, reasonable, required or possible but had no actual understanding of his identity or his greatness, until he heard God's voice. Whether it is Jeremiah hearing God's voice, David hearing God through the prophet Samuel, Moses hearing God in a burning bush, Esther hearing God through her uncle, Joseph hearing God through a dream, or Mary the mother of Jesus hearing God through an angel none of us can come to understand who we truly are or the purpose for which we exist until we hear an announcement from God. The third point I want to make is that God's conversation with Jeremiah announced Jeremiah's Assignment. In the 10th verse of the 1st Chapter of the Book of Jeremiah God spoke to the prophet Jeremiah and declared "See, I have this day set thee over the nations and over the Kingdoms, to root, and to through down, to build, and to plant" I find it interesting how exact God's expression of Jeremiah's ministry was and how little God left to his interpretation. Look at what God declares in verse 9 " then the Lord put forth His, hand, and touched my mouth. And the Lord said unto me, Behold, I have put my words in thy mouth." When God creates us for an assignment He leaves no detail to chance, He arranges each step and each contact to ensure that we have every opportunity to succeed in what he has purposed for us to do. Lets take a look at what the Bible declares in the 26th through 30th verses of the 1st Chapter of the Book of Genesis and 15th through 22nd verses of the 2nd of the Book of Genesis where it provides " And God said, Let us make man in our image, after our likeness: And let them have dominion over the fish of the sea, and over the fowl of the air, and over the cattle, and over all the earth, and over every creepy thing creeth upon the earth. So God created man in His own image, in the image of God created He him; male and female created He them. And God blessed them, and God said unto them, Be fruitful, and multiply, and replenish the earth, and subdue it: and have dominion over the fish of the sea, and over the fowl of the air, and over every living thing that moveth upon the earth. And God said, behold, I have given you every herb hearing seed which is upon the face of all the earth, and every tree in which is the fruit of a tree yielding seed; to you it shall be for meat. And to every beast of the earth, and to every fowl of the air, and to every thing that creepth upon the earth Wherein there is life, I have given every green herb for meat: and it was so.:" and "and the Lord God took the man, and put him into the garden of Eden to dress it and to keep it. And the Lord God commanded the man saying, of every tree of the garden thou mayest freely eat: But of the tree of the knowledge of good and evil, Thou shalt not eat of it: For in the day that thou eatest thereof thou shalt surely die. And the Lord God said, it is not good that the man should be alone; I will make him a help meet for him. And out of the ground the Lord God formed every beast of the field, and every fowl of the air; and brought them unto Adam to see what he would call them: And whatsoever Adam called every living creature, that was the name thereof. And Adam gave names to all the cattle, to the fowl of the air, and to every beast of the field; but for Adam there was not found a help meet for him. And the ribs, and closed up the flesh instead thereof; and the rib, which the Lord God had taken from man, made he a woman and brought her unto the man" these scripture paint an awesome picture of the detail and care God demonstrates as He calls us into the work that He has ordained for us to do for Him. Every instruction provided, every danger exposed, every provision is provided. God leaves nothing to chance and nothing for us to do but follow. Can you imagine Adam trying to subdue the earth without God's instructions, or Noah building the Ark with God's plan, or Moses building the tabernacle of meeting without God's blue print, how about you fulfilling your destiny without God's revelation of your purpose? Where would you begin, how would you or do you know if you are succeeding without a clear understanding of what you are suppose to be succeeding at? As I think about this I am dismayed at the number of members of the Body of Christ who are attempting to lead their lives without God's plan and some how hoping that God will be pleased or that they will succeed. How many have substituted the work that God preordained with the work they themselves have designed, how many who have not yet come to the realization that God has a specific work for them that only they can do.

The second point is that we were created to work under God's direction. As we examine the 5th through 10th verses of the 1st Chapter of the Book of Jeremiah which once again states. "Before I formed thee in the belly I knew thee; and before thou camest forth out of the womb I sanctified thee, and I ordained thee a prophet unto the nations. Then said I, Oh, Lord God: behold, I cannot speak: For I am a child. But the Lord said unto me, say not, I am a child: For thou shalt go to all that I shall send thee, and Be not afraid of their faces: For I am with thee to deliver thee, saith the Lord. Then the Lord put forth His hand, and touched my mouth. And the Lord said unto me, Behold, I have put my words in thy mouth. See, I have this day set thee over the nations and over the Kingdoms, to root out, and to pull down, to build, and to plant." As we look closely at these passages of scripture it is amazing how detailed the Lord's instructions to the Prophet Jeremiah are. These scriptures and more importantly the instructions they convey paint an overwhelmingly clear picture of the partnership that God desires to establish between Himself and His children for the completion of the work that God has assigned each of us. I truly believe that if we are going to succeed in fulfilling the assignment that God has given is it will be important to remember that not only the work itself but also the way the work is done is important to God. Look at what the Apostle Paul teaches us in the 12th through 15th verses of the 3rd Chapter of the 1st Book of Corinthians which reads "Now if any man build upon this foundation gold, silver, precious stones, wood, hay, stubble; Every man's work shall be made manifest: For the day shall declare it, because it shall be revealed by fire; and the fire shall try every man's work of what sort it is, if any man's work abide which he hath built thereupon, he shall receive a reward. If any man's work shall be burned, he shall suffer loss: but he himself shall be saved; yet so as by fire." It is evident from this scripture that not all works are accepted by God and only those which are built with the things of God, (Gold, silver, and precious stones) will endure. One of the major revelations in scripture is that God only accepts what He asks for and everything else is deemed unacceptable. This is the essential lesson we are to learn from the life of Cain. In the 3rd through 7th verses of the 4th Chapter of the Book of Genesis the Bible speaking of Cain declares

"And in process of time it came to pass, that Cain brought of the fruit of the ground an offering unto the Lord. And Abel, he also brought of the first fruit of his flock and of the fat thereof. And the Lord had respect unto Abel to his offering. But unto Cain and to his offering he had not respect. And Cain was very wroth, and his countenance fell. And the Lord said unto Cain, what art thou wroth? And why is thy countenance fallen? If thou doest well, shalt thou not be accepted? And if thou does not well, sin lieth at the door." In other words God will only accept what pleases Him and what pleases Him is what He asks for. Furthermore, in the 5th through 10th verses of the 1st Chapter of the Book of Jeremiah God is very clear about what He is asking for. In these scriptures we see God reserving the right to tell the prophet where to go, to whom to speak, and to give him the words to say, as well as the position to take ("I have this day set thee") and what should result from what is to be said ("to root out, and to pull down, and to destroy, and to throw down, to build and to plant), there was nothing left for Jeremiah to do by to comply. God knew and knows exactly what the right word is at the right time, what word needs to be spoken, when it needs to be spoken, by whom it should be spoken and what should occur as a result of it haven been spoken before He ever commands that it be spoken. However, what is truly sad is the number of people who either find themselves doing their will and offering it to God as a work or attempting to do God's work their way. Both of these situations are sad because they are unnecessary and ineffective resulting in wasted time and damaged lives, destroying not only those that performed these ill-conceived and ill-advised attempts at pleasing God and those who they are intended to impact as well. When I think about those who do this I cannot help but think of what the Bible teaches is in the 5th and 6th verses of the 3rd proverb which declares "Trust in the Lord with all thine heart; and lean not to thy own understanding. In all thy ways acknowledge Him and He will direct thy path." As well as what the Bible declares in the 12th verse of the 14th proverb when it says "There is a way that seemth right unto a man, but the end there of is death." Each of these scriptures should make clear the necessity of not only seeking God's direction but following God's instructions when attempting to do the work that God has assigned each of us as well as the danger of seeking to fulfill God's will our way instead of following God's instructions. The next point I want to make is that our work must rely on God's power. When I think about our need to rely on God's power I cannot help but think about the discussion between Jesus and His disciples found in the 1st Chapter of the Books of Acts. In that discussion the Disciples speaking with Jesus just prior to His ascension into heaven question Him concerning the coming of the Kingdom of God. In the 6th through 8th verses of the 1st Chapter of the Book of acts the Bible states" When they therefore were come together, they asked of Him, saying, Lord, wilt thou at this time restore again the Kingdom to Israel? And He said unto them, it is not for you to know the times or the seasons, which the Father hath put in His own power. But ye shall receive power, after that the Holy Ghost is come upon you: And ye shall be witness unto me both in Jerusalem, and in all Judaea, And in Samaria, and unto the uttermost part of the earth" In this scripture Jesus makes it clear that God's work cannot proceed God's power. There are far too many in the Body of Christ today in leadership positions who are attempting to operate without God's power, having forgotten what Jesus taught us in the 27th verse of the 18th Chapter of the Gospel according to Saint Luke which provides "And He said, the things which are impossible with men are possible with God." This simple but powerful truth is the hallmark of not only the Gospel of our Lord Jesus Christ but the basic of our continued dependence on God. The work that God has assigned each of us is well beyond our human ability, often requires knowledge and wisdom that is beyond human ability to acquire and will ultimately impact people and even nations beyond our ability to imagine. However it is this very fact, our ability to perform a work so much greater than our or any human ability that convinces the world not only that God is with us, but more importantly that God is real, alive and active in the earth. Just imagine the impact the demonstration of God's power had on all of those who watched as Jesus commanded the paralytic to pick up his mat and walk when he rose and walked or the astonishment when the woman with the issue of blood touched the hem of Jesus' garment and was immediately made whole. Would it surprise you to know that demonstrations of God's undeniable power would be just as awe inspiring impactful today as they were in the days in which Jesus walked the earth, that they are just as needed, just as possible today. I realize that for most the prospect of seeing much less performing a miracle, sign or wonder today may seem impossible. But they are just as possible today as they were in the days Jesus walked the earth. Would it surprises you to know that the power to perform such sign and wonders in available to you. In the 12th verse of the 14th Chapter of the Gospel according to Saint John Jesus declared "very, very, I say unto you, He that believeth on me, the works that I do shall he do also; and greater works than these shall he do; because I go unto my Father." In addition, in the 15th through 18th verses of the 16th Chapter of the Gospel according to Saint Mark the Bible declares "And He said unto them, Go ye into all the world, and preach the gospel to every creature. He that believeth and is baptized shall be saved; but he that believeth not shall be dammed. And these signs shall follow them that believe; In my name shall thy cast out devils; they shall speak with new tongues; they shall take up serpent; and if they drink any deadly thing; it shall not hurt them; thy shall lay hands on the sick, and thy shall recover." This scripture is as alive and relevant today as it was when it was spoken and the power of God that was made available to them has also been made available to you today, you must simply believe. We live in a world that is screaming for answers and is disparate for a demonstrate of God's power, a world filled with confusion and in some cases a world without hope and it is your assignment and my assignment to use the power of God to get their attention.

The next point I want to make is our work is to establish God order. In the 28th verse of the 1st Chapter of the Book of Genesis the Bible declares" And God blessed them, and God said unto them, Be fruitful, and Multiply, and replenish the earth, and subdue it: And have dominion over the fish of the sea; and over the fowl of the air, and over every living thing that mouth upon the earth" The word subdue is translated from the Hebrew word "Kalash" which means to tread down, to conquer or to bring into subjection, in short to bring something to order, which is the natural result of exercising dominion over "every living things that moveth upon the earth" I think it should be evident that God who made man in His image and after His likeness intended the order that man established to in the ultimate sense be God's and not man's. I think this is evident in light of the fact that prior to the fall of Adam man had no knowledge apart from God and it was God's spirit that made any activity by Adam possible. In the 7th and 8th verses of the second Chapter of the Book of Genesis the Bible provides "And the Lord God formed man of the dust of the ground, and breathed into his nostrils the breath of life; and man became a living soul and the Lord God planted a garden eastward in Eden; and there He put the man whom he had formed." It is clear from these passages of scripture that man's placement in the garden as well as man's beginning to function in the assignment that God gave him were proceeded by God pouring His spirit into man. The same spirit that now serves as our comforter, our guide, the same spirit that leads us into truth and teaches is to obey the will of God. In addition other scriptural passages clearly establish that our work is to establish God's order. Lets take another look at the word that came to the prophet Jeremiah in the 1st Chapter of the Book of Jeremiah God instructs the prophet Jeremiah where and what to speak but it is the 10th verse God declares "see I have this day set thee over the nations and over the Kingdoms, to root out, and to pull down, and to destroy, and to throw down, to build, and to plant." Do you see the picture of God using the prophet

Jeremiah to establish God's order? How God specifically chooses the words Jeremiah is to speak and the places he will speaks them and determine what will happen as a result, all based on God's intended result. The picture that the Bible paints of the assignment that God gave the prophet Jeremiah is typical of the assignment that God has given to all of His servant including you and I. It is in essence to speak the words that God places in our mouth or take the actions that God directs so that the result that God intends will occur. It is not God's intent that you nor I decide for ourselves what we should say, or do when we should say it or what we should intend to accomplish and those who do, do so at great peril. One of the clearest examples of this is found in the 29th Chapter of the Book of Jeremiah. In the 8th and 9th verses of the 29th Chapter of the Book of Jeremiah the Bible declares " For thus saith the Lord of hosts, the God of Israel; Let not your prophets and your diviners, that be in the midst of you, deceive you, neither hearken to your dreams which ye cause to be dreamed. For they prophecy falsely unto you in my name: I have not sent them, saith the Lord." And in the 30th through 32nd verses of the 29th Chapter of the Book of Jeremiah saying, send to all them of the captivity, saying, thus saith the Lord concerning Shemaiah, the Nehelanite; Because that Shemaiah has prophesied unto you, and I sent him not and he caused you to trust a lie: Therefore, thus saith the Lord; Behold I will punish Shemaiah the Nehelanite, and his seed: he shall not have a man to dwell among this people; neither shall he behold the good that I will do my people; saith the Lord; because he hath taught rebellion against the Lord." I think one of the most important understandings any Christian can have is articulated in these passage of scripture, we are either establishing God's order or we are establishing rebellion against it and there is no middle ground. One of the most horrible things about this truth is that we can establish people in rebellion and not even realize that we are doing it until it is too late. Every time we as Christian speak we are seen as speaking on God's behalf and those we speak to assume what we say is God will and God's intention so if we speak words that God has not put in our mouth we are creating something that God did not intend and leading people astray.

The last point I want to make is our work is based on God's timing. It should go without saying that God's timing is perfect. Each and every assignment is perfectly timed by God to ensure that each party involved will receive exactly what is needed to move God's will forward. In the 1st Chapter of the Book of Genesis the Bible teaches us that God created the heavens and the earth and over those six days establish each form of life in the exact order so that each act of creation would support the next. For example God separated the firmament and separated the land from the seas before He created fish, created trees before He created birds all of which was perfectly timed to produce exactly what God intended. As it is with God's work so it with ours. The word time or times appears some 768 times in the word of God almost twice as many times as the word love, more than four times as many times as the word money and almost twice as many times as the word faith. If we were to examine the first Chapter of the Book of Genesis as I mentioned earlier we would see that every act in God's plan of creation was strategically done both in terms of its relation one to another and in terms of it individual function, even the creation of man and his placement in the garden was timed so that everything over which he was given dominion was established and in position prior to his arrival. This facet of

God's timing is demonstrated through scripture, one of the clearest examples of this is found in the story Ester. In the 14th verse of the 4th chapter of the Book of Ester the Bible recounts a conversation between Ester and her uncle mordecai that speaks volumes to both the necessity and the timing of the work God assigns to us, when it provides." For if thou altogether holdest thy peace at this time, then shall the enlargement and deliverance arise to the Jews from another place; but thou and thy father's house shall be destroy: and who knoweth whether thou art come to the Kingdom for such a time as this?" In this scripture mordecai raises issues that I believe each of us need to address, how the timing of God's actions relate to the purpose of our lives. For many, even in the Body of Christ, they see the events in their lives as random and unrelated, never recognizing or even considering the divine orchestration of their lives. When I think about the life of

Ester, the life of Moses the life of Joseph and so many others I hear the Apostle Paul speaking in the 28th the verse of the 8th chapter of the Book of Romans when he said "and we know that all things work together for good to them that love God, to them who are the called according to his purpose." Because every action is deigned or permitted by God to place us in the right condition at the right moment and in the right place to fulfill the next piece of work God has assigned to us. Without God's direction, God's preparation and God's prompting succeeding in the things of God, the work which we have been assigned would not be possible. Lets look once more at what the Lord spoke to the prophet Jeremiah in the 7th through 10th verses of the 1st Chapter of the Book of Jeremiah "But the Lord said unto me say not, I am a child: For thou shalt go to all that I shall send thee, and whatsoever I command thee thou shall speak, Be not afraid of their faces: For I am with thee to deliver thee, saith the Lord, then the Lord put forth his hand, and touched my mouth, and the Lord said unto me behold, I have put my words in thy mouth. See I have this day set thee over the nations and over the Kingdoms, to root out, and to pull down, and to destroy, and to throw down, to build, and to plant." In this scripture it becomes clear that God seek to establish the timing for the fulfillment of each stage of Jeremiah's ministry and there was nothing left for him to do but obey, just as it was with Jeremiah so too is it with us, each event, each aspect of the work we have been assigned is to be determined by God.

4.

ELEMENT FOUR

The believer's understanding that God has given them gift and abilities which God intends the believers to use in His Kingdom and it is their responsibility to discover, desire, cultivate and develop and activate them.

In the 1st and 2nd verse of the 12th Chapter of the Book of Genesis the Bible speaking of God's conversation with Abram provides "Now the Lord had said unto Abram, get thee out of thy country, and from thy kindred, and from thy father house, unto a land that I will shew thee and I will make of thee a great nation, and I will bless thee, and make thy name great; and thou shalt be a blessing." In this scripture God reveals His plan to create a nation unto His self, a nation which through His direction would become great among men and in so doing demonstrate the greatness of God. I find it interesting that when God decided to form a nation He did call a group of people, or even a family but a single man who was past his prime, who was not famous or even important in the society he lived in and but possessed two traits of interest to God, the ability to hear and willingness to believe, everything else that he needed would be provided by God. I think it is even more interesting that the two things Abram needed to fulfill his destiny and his role in the establishment of God's Kingdom on the earth were both gifts given to him by God, the gift of prophecy and the gift of faith.

I realize that many if not most who read the story of Abram would not readily think of Abram as a prophet or perhaps I should say as one who operated in the gift of prophecy. However, our failure to recognize Abram's gift has more to do with how the modern Church has taught us to see the gift and office of the prophet than it does whether Abram actually possessed the gifts. In the modern church we see prophets or those who operate in the gift of prophecy as those who declare God's word on a regular basis and as such focus on their speaking, however I think it would be more appropriate to focus on their hearing. I think at lease most would agree that a prophet cannot speak God's word if they cannot first hear God's word and as such I believe the measure of a prophet lies more in the hearing (or I should say discerning) than in the speaking, and there is no doubt that Abram heard God's voice as God instructed Abram to "Get thee out of thy country, and from thy kindred, and from they father's house, unto a land I will show thee" (Gen 12:1) or when God expressed his intentions towards Abram In the 2nd and 3rd verse of the 12th Chapter of the Book of Genesis when He declared "and I will make of thee a great nation, and I will bless thee, and make thy name great; and thou shalt be a blessing: and I will bless them that bless thee, and curse him that curseth thee: and in thee shall all the families of the earth be blessed" In addition, if we were to examine the subsequent Chapters of the Book of Genesis as well as both the Book of Exodus and the Book of Numbers it would become evident that not only did Abram hear God's words but he declared them to both Sarah and Isaac as well. The fact that Abram operated in the gift of faith is also supported by scripture when the Bible declares in the 4th verse of the 12th Chapter of the Book of Genesis "So Abram departed, as the Lord had spoken unto him" When I think about this scripture I think about what the Apostle James teaches us about faith in the 14th through 17th verses of the 2nd Chapter of the Book of James when He declared "What doth it profit, my brethren through a man say he hath faith, and have not works? Can faith save him? If a brother or sister be naked, and destitute of daily food, and one of you say unto them, depart in peace, be ye warmed and filled; notwithstanding ye give them not those things which are needful to the body; what doth it profit? Even so faith, it hath not works, is dead, being alone." Therefore Abrams faith was clearly established not only to exist but to be alive when he chose to obey and follow God. I wonder if we were to examine our faith under the lens of the Apostle James' statement how alive out faith would prove to be. However, despite how alive Abram's faith was when he set out to follow God, his faith like all gifts we receive from God needed to be cultivated, developed and put into use for God. It is clear from the 4th verse of the 12th Chapter of the Book of Genesis that Abram was given the gift of faith from God in fact the Bible on a number of occasions speaks of Abram's faith and hold it up as a standard for the rest of us to follow. One such example of the Bible using Abram's faith as a standard is found in the 8th through 10 verses of the 11th Chapter of the Book of Hebrews where the Apostle Paul speaking on the importance of faith wrote " By faith Abraham, when he was called to go out into a place which he should after receive for an inheritance, obeyed; and he went out, not knowing wither he went; By faith he sojourned on the land of promise as in a strange country, dwellings in tabernacles with Isaac and Jacob, the heirs with him of the same promise: For he looked for a city which hath foundations, whose builder and maker is God "And in the 11th verse of the 11th Chapter of the Book of Hebrews speaking of Sarah declared "through faith also Sara herself received strength to conceive seed and was delivered of a child when see was past age, because she judged him faithful who had promised." It is equally clear from scripture that the magnitude of faith Abram operated in developed over time. The 4th through 9th verses of the 12th Chapter of the Book of Genesis provides us with a clear example of this point when it provides " So Abram departed, as the Lord had spoken unto him; and Lot went with him: And Abram was seventy and five years old when he departed out of Haran. And Abram took Sarai his wife, and Lot his brother's son and all their substance that they had gathered, and the souls that they had gotten in Haran; and they went forth to go into the land of Canaan; and in the land of Canaan they came. And Abram passed through the land unto the place of Sichen, unto the plain of Moreh. And the Canaanites were then in the land, And the Lord appeared unto Abram, and said unto thy seed will I give this land: And there build he an alter unto the Lord, who appeared unto him. And he removed from thence unto a mountain on the east of Bethel, and pitched his tent, having Bethel on the west and Hai on the east: and there he built an alter unto the Lord, and called upon the name of the Lord. And Abram journeyed, going on still towards the south. And there was a famine in the land: and Abram went down into Egypt to sojourn there; for the famine was grievous in the land" do you see the frailty of Abram's faith, how Abram allowed fear to overwhelm his faith and drive him out of position to receive his promise? Do you see the hand of the enemy trying to destroy Abram's faith and render the gift that God gave Abram useless for the building of God's Kingdom on the earth. I wonder how many times the enemy has caused an event or situation to occur that overwhelmed our faith and drove us out of position and endangered our promise, how many times our destiny has been delayed if not lost because we like Abram, in this scripture, responded to a test with fear and not faith. As I examine this scripture I am amazed at the price Abram paid and we pay each and every day, because he responded in fear. This point is made even clearer in the 11th through 15th verses of the 12th Chapter of the Book of Genesis which provides "And it came to pass, when he was come near to enter into Egypt, that he said into Sarai his wife, Behold now I know that thou art a fair woman to look upon: therefore it shall come to pass, when the Egyptians shall see thee that they shall say this is his wife: and they will kill me, but they will save thee alive say I pray thee, that thou are my sister: that it may be well with me for thy sake; and my soul shall live because of thee. And it came to pass, that, when Abram was come into Egypt; the Egyptians beheld the woman that she was very fair. The princes also of Pharaoh: And the woman was taken into Pharaoh's house." I find it interesting how when our faith is overwhelmed by fear the actions we take to protect and provide for ourselves seek to rob us of the very things we need to walk in God's promises for us. I wonder how many times we have found ourselves in a situation much like Abrams, the specifics many be different but the underlying circumstances are the same. We hear a promise or a command from the Lord and receive it with great faith and joy, immediately responding in faith, then suddenly just as we are positioned for victory a test of our faith comes in the form of a challenge or and outright attack, what do we do, stand our ground in faith, believing that God can handle the situation or do we do as Abram did when he was faced with his, and allow fear to cause us to move out of position and in so doing risk the very things that are necessary for the promise we are standing believing in God to bring to pass. I think it is worth mentioning that whenever God makes a promise the enemy is going to launch an attack and the effectiveness of the attack will be determined by how much we have cultivated and developed our faith. However, one of the many things that I love about God is that He is faithful to us even when we are not faithful to Him, even when our faith fails. Look at how God intervenes in the 17th through 20th verses of the 12th Chapter of the Book of Genesis which provides "And the Lord plagued Pharaoh and his house with great plagues because of Sarai Abram's wife. And Pharaoh called Abram and said what is this that thou hast done unto me? Why didst thou not tell me that she was thy wife? Why saidst thou she is my sister? So I might have taken her to me to wife: now therefore behold thy wife take her and go thy way. And Pharaoh commanded his men concerning him: that they sent him away, and his wife, and all that he had." Isn't it amazing how faithful God was to His promise despite Abram's failure, but isn't that the first lesson we need to learn to truly develop our faith, that God's promises are based on who He is and not who we are, based on His character and not ours. As I read verse 17 I cannot help but hear God's words to Abram in the 3rd verse of the 12th Chapter of the Book of Genesis when God declared "And I will bless them that bless thee, and curse them that curse them that curse thee." Just imagine the lesson Abram learned as he saw God put His power behind His promise. This point, that faith requires trust in God's power is one of the three major keys to developing our faith that we learn from the life of Abram. The second as we shall see next is the need to trust God's timing. In the 1st through 3rd verses of the 15th Chapter of the Book of Genesis we see what we should recognize as a very common discussion between God and someone standing in God's promises. The 1st through 3rd verses of the 15th Chapter of the Book of Genesis reads "After these things the word of the Lord came unto Abram in a vision, saying, fear not, Abram: I am thy shield, and thy exceedingly great reward. And Abram said Lord, what wilt thou give me, seeing I go childless and the steward of my house is this Eliezer of Damascus? And Abram said, behold, to me thou hast given no seed: and lo, one born in my house is mine heir." In this scripture we see Abram dealing with one of the greatest challenges that those of us who live in faith face, God's timing. Imagine Abram, having heard God's promise of not only a seed, but of a great nation, an entire community of people who are to be descendants of his seed, think of the joy and excitement as he heard God's promise and set out in faith anticipating the immediate move of God. Have you ever been there, in that place of expectation having heard a word from the Lord promising to provide something so important to you that it taps into your very core only to watch day after day, week after week, month after month and even year after year go by without so much as a shred of evidence that the promise will come to pass much less when, If you have then I am sure you can understand how Abram must have felt, getting up in age, unsure how much longer he or Sarai would live, realizing that she was already past the age where conception was possible. I can picture Abram, rehearsing the initial conversation with God in his mind over and over again, examining every detail searching for evidence that it was real or in the alternative any detail that he may have missed that might provide him with some comfort that it is not too late and the promise is still possible. Perhaps even a key instruction he might have missed that may explain what he must have seemed as a delay. This is what it is like to struggle with the timing of God, it is not easy but at one point or another we will all have to do it, because God's timing and our timing are rarely the same, the key is not to allow the delay to damage your faith. In the 12th verse of the 13th proverb the Bible declares "hope deferred maketh the heart sick: but when the desire cometh, it is a tree of life" and I believe that this scripture describes exactly how Abram felt, sick in his heart. I would be, wouldn't you? But God whose timing is always perfect, comes to comfort Abram in the 4th and 5th verses of the 15th Chapter of the Book of Genesis which says: And behold, the word of the Lord came unto him saying, this shall not be thine heir; but he that shall come forth out of thine own bowels shall be thine heir. And he brought him forth abroad, and said; Look now towards heaven, and tell the stars, if thou be able to number them: and he said unto him, so shall thy seed be." In this scripture God's responds to Abram's concerns by reaffirming His promise to Abram and in response to Abram's faith God goes even further by revealing details about God's promise and God's plan. Take a look at the 7th through 17th verses of the 15th Chapter of the Book of Genesis which provides "And He said unto him, I am the

Lord that brought thee out of Ur of the Chaldees, to give thee this land to inherit it. And He said, Lord God whereby shall I know that I shall inherit it? And He said unto him, take me a heifer of three years old, and a she goat of three years old, and a ram of three years old, and a turtledove, and a young pigeon. And he took unto him all these, and divided them in the midst, and laid each piece one against another: but the birds divided he not. And when the fowls came down upon the carcasses, Abram drove them away. And when the sun was going down, a deep sleep fell upon Abram; and lo, a horror of great darkness fell upon him. And he said unto Abram, know of a surety that thy seed shall be a stranger in a land that is not theirs, and shall serve them; and they shall afflict them four hundred years; and also that nations, whom they serve, will I judge: and afterwards shall they come out with great substance. And thou shalt go to thy fathers in peace. Thou shalt be buried in a good old age. But in the fourth generation they shall come hither again: for the iniquity of the Amorites is not yet full. And it came to pass that when the sun went down, and it was dark, behold a smoking furnace, and a burning lamp that passed between those pieces." In these passages of scripture we see God respond to Abram's concerns over what he perceives as a delay in the performance of God's word with a revelation of God's plan and things to come. I think it is amazing how God validates His word with His word, because there is nothing greater that God could use, it is important to note, however, that God did not offer to change His timing to adjust to Abram's expectations but rather required Abram to adjust his expectations to line up with God's timing. Whenever we run short of patience God's response will serve to give us the confidence to wait and in so doing help us to develop faith not just in His promise but also in His timing.

The third area where God will develop our gift of faith is in the area of His ways. In the 1st through 6th verses of the 16th Chapter of the Book of Genesis the Bible declares "Now Sarai Abram's wife bare him no children: and she had a handmaid, an Egyptian whose name was Hagar. And Sarai said unto Abram, behold now, the Lord hath restrained me from bearing: I pray thee go into my handmaid; it may be that I may obtain children by her. And Abram hearkened to the voice of Sarai. And Sarai Abram's wife took Hagar her maid the Egyptian, after Abram dwelt ten years in the land of Canaan and gave her to her husband to wife. And he went in unto Hagar, and she conceived: and when she saw that she conceived, her mistress was displeased in her eyes, and Sarai said unto Abram. My wrong be upon thee: I have given my maid into thy bossom; and when she saw that she had conceived, I was despised in her eyes: the Lord judge between me and thee. But Abram said to Sarai, behold, thy maid is in thy hands; do to her as it pleaseth thee. And when Sarai dealt harshly with her, she fled from her face." I trust that it goes without saying that it was not God's will that the seed God promised to Abram be produced through Hagar but through Sarai. I also trust it is equally clear that whenever we attempt to assist God in the fulfillment of His promises through our means disaster results. As I contemplate the decision of Sarai and Abram to assist God, I cannot help but hear the 25th verse of the 16th proverb which states "There is a way that seemeth right unto man, but the end thereof are the ways of death." Have you ever considered the consequences of the decision they made while trying to fulfill God's promise in the way that seemed right to them, when I think about it I am horrified at the magnitude of the death that resulted. The plain hard truth is that had Abram not taken Hagar as his wife, their seed Ishmael would have never been born, had there been no Ishmael there would be no Islam and had there been no Islam there world would have been spare terrorism as we have tragically come to know it. Just imagine the lives that have been lost and the families shattered as a result of a single decision to attempt to fulfill God's promises with man's means. It is easy to understand how this could happen and if we are honest with ourselves we have done or at least been tempted to do the same thing countless times. From Abram and Sarai's point of view, (as often is ours) their underlying premise made complete sense, the ends justify the means, God said Abram was to be the father of many nations and that his heir was going to come from his seed, so what difference does it make if they intervene. After all it has been ten long years, if God was going to do something surely He would have done it by now. We are not getting any younger and we cannot let what might be our only "realistic" opportunity pass us by. While this process of analysis is quite human it is not God! In the 8th and 9th verses of the 55th Chapter of the Book of Isaiah God declared "For my thoughts are not your thoughts; neither are your ways my ways, saith the Lord. For as the heavens are higher than the earth, so are my ways higher than your ways, and my thoughts than your thoughts." Or as the Apostle Paul wrote in the 7th verse of the 8th Chapter of the Book of Romans "because the carnal mind is enmity against God: for it is not subject to the laws of God, neither indeed can be." It should come as no surprise that we cannot think like God or even truly understand how or what God thinks. So then why does attempting to fulfill God's promises our way have such an appeal to us. Is it impatience, pride, ignorance or are we simply unaware if God's true intent? God who is fully aware of all information at all times knew that Sarai's season of child baring had passed before He spoke the promise of a seed to Abram. Therefore He would not have spoken the promise if her condition would have been a hindrance. In addition, had God so required He could have called Abram when Sarai was still of child baring age, but He chose not to, but rather to wait until the possibility of producing a seed naturally had expired. But the question is why? Why would God wait so long until the chances are so dim, when it seemed so impossible? The answer is simple and is found in a statement made by the Apostle Paul in the 6th verse of the 11th Chapter of the Book of Hebrews "without faith it is impossible to please God." And the gift of faith like every other gift must be cultivated and developed and that is only possible is the gift is actually used. But faith is only needed when human ability and reason fail, faith only flourishes in an environment where the impossible needs to be performed.

But faith is not the only gift that needs to be cultivated and developed as we will see as we examine the life of Joseph. I would imagine that virtually everyone in the Body of Christ if not everyone in the world knows the story of Joseph contained in the 37th through 50th Chapters of the Book of Genesis. The story of how Jacob's youngest son went from shepherd to the de facto king of Egypt and in so doing saved the nations of Israel and the Egypt from starvation. However, what is perhaps not as well known is how Joseph cultivation, development and use of his God given gifts positioned Joseph to fulfill his destiny. In the 5th through 14th verses of the 37th Chapter of the Book of Genesis the Bible provides " And Joseph dreamed a dream, and he told it to his brethren: and they hated him yet the more and he said unto them, hear, I pray you, this dream which I have dreamed: For behold, we were binding sheaves in the field, and lo, my sheaf arose, and also stood upright; and, behold, your sheaves stood round about, and made obedience to my sheaf. And his brethren said to him, shalt thou indeed reign over us? Or shalt thou indeed have dominion over us? And the hated him yet the more for his dreams, and for his words. And he dreamed yet another dream, and told it to his brethren, and said behold, I have dreamed a dream more; and behold the sun and the moon and the eleven stars made obeisance to me. And he told it to his father, and his brethren: and his father rebuked him, and said unto him, what is this dream that thou has dreamed? Shall I and thy mother and thy brethren indeed come to bow down ourselves to thee to the earth? And his brethren envied him; but his father observed the saying and his brethren went to feed their father's flock in Shechem. And Israel said unto Joseph, do not thy brethren feed the flock in Shechem? Come, and I will send thee unto them, and he said to him, here am I. And he said to him, go I pray thee, see whether it be well with thy brethren, and well with the flock; and bring me word again. So he sent him out of the vale of Hebron, and he came to Shechem." In this passage of scripture we see several of Joseph's gifts spring forth. We see Joseph's gift of prophecy, his gift of administration (or ruler ship as it is sometimes called), his gift of faith, and as we move through our discussion we will see his gift of mercy (or compassion as it is sometimes called). Each of these gifts were given to Joseph by God, just as they are given to each of us, because they are necessary tools in the fulfillment of Joseph's assignment and each must be cultivated and developed in order to be put to use for God. Most of us, at first glance would not think of Joseph as a prophet but in the 5th through 7th verses of the 37th Chapter of the book of Genesis we see God giving Joseph a prophetic vision of his position in the Kingdom and the role he was destine to play in its protection and deliverance from destruction due to the famine which was to come. Moreover in the 9th verse of the 37th Chapter of the Book of Genesis which provides "And he dreamed yet another dream, and told it his brethren, and said behold I have dreamed a dream more; and behold the sun and the moon and the eleven stars made obeisance to me" we see that Joseph initial dream was not an one time occurrence but rather was a consistent part of how God used Joseph to bring deliverance to God's people. In addition to the gift of prophecy we also see Joseph's gift of faith in Joseph's willingness to proclaim the visions that God gave him in spite the ridicule he would face or the rejection he would encounter. It is interesting that Joseph like many prophets find themselves facing rejection and even hatred by the very people that God uses them to save and the ability to stand and declare the word of God or in Joseph's case the vision given him by God is a test of one's faith. Listen to what the 4th through 11th verses of the 37th Chapter of the Book of Genesis say concerning Joseph relationship with his family "and when his brethren saw that their father loved him more than all his brethren, they hated him, and could not speak peaceably unto him. And Joseph dreamed a dream, and he told it his brethren: and they hated him yet the more. And he said unto then, hear I pray you this dream which I have dreamed: For, behold, we were binding sheaves in the field, and lo my sheaf arose, and also stood upright; and, behold, your, sheaves stood around about and made obeisance to my sheaf. And his brethren said to him; shalt thou indeed reign over us? And thy hated him yet the more for his dream, and for his words. And he dreamed yet another dream, and told it his brethren, and said, behold, I have dreamed a dream more; and, behold, the sum and the moon and the eleven star made obeisance to me, and he told it to his father, and to his brethren: and his father rebuked him and said unto him, what is this dream that thou hast dreamed? Shall I and thy mother and thy brethren indeed come to bow down ourselves to thee to the earth?" In these scriptures we see Joseph face a series of tests of his faith and his commitment to cultivate and use the gift of prophecy given to him by God. For those who God has graced with a prophetic gift whether in the form of an office of a prophet found in the 4th verse of the 11th Chapter of the Book of Ephesians, the gift of prophecy, word of wisdom, word of knowledge, gift of prophecy or gift of discernment found in the 8th through 10th verses of the 12th Chapter of the Book of 1st Corinthians or the gift of prophecy found in the 6th verse of the 12th chapter of the Book of Romans it is quite often difficult to face the ridicule and rejection that comes along with God's use of these gifts and it takes a considerable amount of faith to declare God's word or share a vision especially to those they know, much less live with. This was especially true of Joseph. As I read these passages of scripture I was amazed at how Joseph continued to reveal the visions God gave him in the face of his families continued rejection and his brother's escalating hatred towards him. It is even more amazing to me that God knowing the hatred he faced would not only continue to give Joseph visions of their future submission to him but would give him visions that were increasingly clear and created a shaper and more undeniable picture of the future relationship between Joseph and the members of Joseph's family. The reason for this lies in the fact that faith is only developed under pressure and the gift of prophecy is developed by frequency of its usage and is often sharpened in opposition or adverse circumstances.

In addition to the gift of faith and the gift of prophecy we see in Joseph the gift of administration (or ruler ship as it is sometimes called) without which the gift of prophecy possessed by Joseph would have served no purpose. Joseph's gift of administration is first demonstrated in the 12th through 17th verses of the 37th Chapter of the Book of Genesis which provides "And his brethren went to feed their father's flock in shechem. And Israel said unto Joseph, do not thy brethren feed the flock in Shechem? Come, and I will send thee unto them, and he said to him, here am I. And he said to him, Go, I pray thee see whether it be well with thy brethren and well with the flocks; and bring me word again, So he sent him out of the vale of Hebron, and he came to shechem, and a certain man found him. And behold, he was wondering in the field: and the man asked him. Saying, what seekest thou? And He said, I seek my brethren: tell me, I pray thee, where they feed their flocks. And the man said. They are departed hence; for I heard them saying, Let us go to Dothan. And Joseph went after his brethren, and found them in Dothan." In find it interesting how Joseph's father could rebuke Joseph for having a vision of being in a position of authority in one breath and then place him in a position of authority in the next. I find it even more interesting how diligently Joseph searched for his brothers seeking to determine the safety of his brothers who hated him so intensely and demonstrated it so publically, but that is the true test of spiritual maturity and spiritual leadership. The willingness to do what is right when you may not desire it and when those who benefit from it do not deserve it. The gift of administration like the gift of prophecy are cultivated through their use and developed through adversity. In the 6th through 20th verses of the 39th Chapter of the Book of Genesis the Bible paints a picture of what it means to operate in adversity when speaking of Joseph it provides "And he left all that he had in Joseph's hands; and he knew not ought he had, save the bread which he did eat. And Joseph was a goodly person, and well favored. And it came to pass after these things, that his master's wife cast her eyes upon Joseph; and she said, lie with me. But he refused, and said unto his master's wife, behold, my master wotteth not what is with me in the house, and he hath committed all that he hath to my hand; there is none greater in his house than I; neither hath he kept back any thing from me but thee, because thou art his wife: how then can I do this great wickedness, and sin against God? And it came to pass, as she spake to Joseph day by day that he harkened not unto her, to be by her, or to be with her. And it came to pass about this time that Joseph went into the house to do his business; and there was none of the men of the house there within and she caught him by his garment, saying lie with me: and he left his garment in her hand, and fled, and got him out. And it came to pass, when she saw that he had left his garment in her hand, and was fled that she called unto the men of the house, and spake unto them, saying, see he hath brought in an Hebrew unto us to mock us; he came in unto me to lie with me, and I cried with a loud voice: and it came to pass, when he heard that I lifted up my voice and cried, that he left his garment with me, and fled, and got him out. And she laid up his garment by her until his lord came home. And she spake unto him according to these words, saying the Hebrew servant, which thou hast brought unto us, came in unto me to mock me: and it came to pass, as I lifted up my voice and cried, that he left his garment with me, and fled out. And it came to pass, when his master heard the words of his wife, which she spake unto him; saying after this manner did thy servant to me; that his wrath was kindled. And Joseph's master took him, and put him into the prison, a place where the king's prisoners were bound: and he was there in the prison." Can you imagine what it would be like to find yourself in Joseph's shoes. First you are betrayed by your brothers and sold into slavery simply because you told them about a vision given to you by God. Then you find yourself in the service of an extremely powerful man and given the responsibility of managing everything he owns. I realize that at first glance this may seem like a dream come true, but have you ever work for a person of great power, one who is use to getting what they want when they want it and how they want it, the type of person who has likely never heard the word no, or at least not from the same person twice. A person with so much power that, a changer in their mood, much less their opinion of you, could change the course and perhaps even the longevity of your life. When it comes to situations like this things are not always what they appear to be. Just imagine the pressure to perform, and make sure that everything is accounted for. Now add to that the pressure and for that matter the danger of dealing with his wife. A woman who has no respect for her husband or his position and is only interested in getting what she wants and what she wants is you. So how do you deal with the pressure of appeasing him and resisting her? How do you deal with the advances day after day? How do you balance your need to perform with you're your need to protect yourself and maintain your integrity when you are being pulled and tempted by sin everyday? How do you keep your focus in the face of sometimes overwhelming and never ending distractions knowing that if you slip everything you hope to accomplish can be destroyed in the blink of an eye? This was the test and the temptation that Joseph faced and this is the place where his gift of administration was developed and his character was tested, but what about you? What seemingly impossible situations have you found yourself in, situations in which everything seems to hinge on what actions you take each day, in short how are you being tested? As I prepare to conclude this Chapter I want to turn your attention to the life of David. I think everyone recognizes that David was a great King and an epic figure in Biblical history but I question how many have ever considered what spiritual gifts David possessed that led to his greatness or recognize the fact that David's spiritual gifts, like ours had to be cultivated and developed in order for them to be used for God's glory.

In the 14th through 23rd verses of the 16th Chapter of the 1st Book of Samuel the Bible paints an interesting portrait of David when it provides "But the spirit of the Lord departed from Saul, and an evil spirit from the Lord troubled him. And Saul's servant said unto him, behold now, an evil spirit from the Lord troubleth thee. Let our lord command thy servants, which are before thee, to seek out a man, who is a cunning player on a harp: And it shall come to pass, when the evil spirit from God is upon thee, that he shall play with his hand, and thou shalt be well. And Saul said unto his servants, provide me now a man that can play well, and bring him to me. Then answered one of the servants, and said, behold I have seen a son of Jessie the Beth-lehemite, that is cunning in playing, and a mighty valiant man, and a man of war, and prudent in matters, and a comely person, and the Lord is with him. Wherefore Saul sent messengers unto Jessie and said, send me David thou son, which is with the sheep. And Jessie took an ass laden with bread, and a bottle of wine, and a kid, and sent then by David his son unto Saul. And David came to Saul, and stood before him: and he loved him greatly; and he became his Armorbearers. And Saul sent to Jessie, saying, Let David, I pray thee, stand before me; for he hath found favor in my sight. And it came to pass, when the evil spirit from God was upon Saul, that David took a harp, and played with his hand: so Saul was refreshed, and well, and the evil spirit departed from him." As I read this passage of scripture I cannot help but hear what the Bible says in the 16th verse of the 18th proverb where it states "A man's gifts maketh room for him, and bringeth him before great men" because that is exactly what happen to David, David's gift of exhortation (or encouragement as it is sometimes called) was so well know that it brought him before King Saul, and there was no man greater than King Saul in all of Israel. However, David's gifts, just like Joseph's just like Abram's, just like yours and mine, needed to be cultivated and developed in order for God to use them for His ultimate glory and the gift of exhortation like every other gift is cultivated by use and developed through adversity and David was no stranger to adversity.

In the 7th through 13th verses of the 18th Chapter of the 1st Book of Samuel we see the adversity that David would face take shape for the Bible declares "And the women answered one another as they played, and said, Saul hath slain his thousands, and David his ten thousands. And Saul was very wroth, and the saying displeased him; and he said they have ascribed unto David ten thousands, and to me they have ascribed but thousands: and what can he have more but the kingdom? And Saul eyed David from that day and forward. And it came to pass on the morrow that the evil spirit from God came upon Saul, and he prophesied in the midst of the house: And David played with his hand, as at other times: and there was a javelin, for he said, I will smite David even to the wall with it. And David avoided out of his presence twice. And Saul was afraid of David, because the Lord was with him, and was departed from Saul. Therefore Saul removed him from him, and made him captain over a thousand; and he went out and came in before the people." Think about how David must have felt as he dogged the Javelin Saul threw at him, how his heart must have sunk into the pit of his stomach and fear rose in his heart. To make matters worse the person who has become so enraged that he desires to take his life is the King. What do you do when the King develops a hatred towards you simply because of who God made you to be and your only crime is being gifted? I am sure there are many people in the Body of Christ who are facing this very situation, their boss or even their pastor has taken a dislike to them simply because God has blessed them with a gift and it seems like the more you try or the better you perform the worse your situation gets. Well maybe, just maybe you find yourself in the situation you are in because God is developing your gifts to use you for something greater. For those of you who may be facing this situation I want to remind you of an observation that Joseph made about his brother's treatment of him which is found in the 19th and 20th verses of the 50th Chapter of the Book of Genesis where he said " fear not: for am I in the place of God? But as for you, ye thought evil against me; but God meant it unto good, to bring to pass, as it is this day, to save much people alive" or as the Apostle Paul wrote in the 28th verse of the 8th Chapter of the Book of Romans which provides " and we know that all things work together for good to them that love God, to them who are the called according to his purpose" While it is clear from scripture that Saul meant David evil we know that every thing that David experienced God used for David's good because in the midst of all that David went through God was developing David's gifts and preparing David for his destiny. Take a closer look at the adversity David faced at the hands of Saul and how David responded. In the 14th verse of the 18th Chapter through the 11th verse of the 19th Chapter of the 1st Book of Samuel the Bible tells the story of Saul's treatment of David and provides "And David behaved himself wisely in all his ways; and the Lord was with him. Wherefore when Saul saw that he behaved himself very wisely, he was afraid of him. But all Israel and Judah loved David, because he went out and came in before them. And Saul said to David, behold my elder daughter Merab, her will I give thee to wife: only be thou valiant for me, and fight the LORD'S battles. For Saul said, Let not mine hand be upon him, but let the hand of the Philistines be upon him. And David said unto Saul, who am I? And what is my life. Or my father's family in Israel, that I should be son in law to the king? But it came to pass at the time when Merab Saul"s daughter should have been given to David, that she was given unto Adriel the Metholathite to wife. And Michal Saul's daughter loved David: and they told Saul, and the thing pleased him. And Saul said, I will give him her, that she may be a snare to him, and that the hand of the Philistines may be against him. Wherefore Saul said to David, Thou shalt this day be my son in law in the one of the twain. And Saul commanded his servants, saying, Commune with David secretly, and say, Behold, the king hath delight in thee, and all his servants love thee: now therefore be the king's son in law, and Saul's servants spake those words in the ears of David. And David said, Seemeth it to you a light thing to be a king's son in law, seeing that I am a poor man, and lightly esteemed? And the servants of Saul told him, saying, on this manner spake David. And Saul said thus shall ye say to David, The king desireth not any dowry, but a hundred foreskins of the Philistines, to be avenged of the king's enemies. But Saul thought to make David fall by the hand of the Philistines. And when his servants told David these words, it pleased David well to be the king's son in law: and the days were not expired. Wherefore David arose and went, he and his men, and slew of the Philistines two hundred men; and David brought their foreskins, and they gave them in full tale to the king, that he might be the king's son in law. And Saul gave him Michal his daughter to wife. And Saul saw and knew that the Lord was with David, and that Michal Saul's daughter loved him. And Saul was yet the more afraid of David; and Saul became David's enemy continually. Then the princes of the Philistines went forth: and it came to pass, after they went forth, that David behaved more wisely than all the servants of Saul; so that his name was much set by. And Saul spake to Jonathan his son, and to all his servants, that they should kill David. But Jonathan Saul's son delighted much in David: and Jonathan told David, saying Saul my father seeketh to kill thee: now therefore, I pray thee, take heed to thyself until morning, and abide in a secret place, and hide thyself: And I will go out and stand beside my father in the field where thou art, and I will commune with my father of thee; and what I see, that I will tell thee. And Jonathan spake good of David unto Saul his father, and said unto him, Let not the king sin against his servant, against David; because he hath not sinned against thee, and because his works have been to thee-ward very good: For he did put his life in his hand, and slew the Philistine, and the Lord wrought a great salvation for all Israel: thou sawest it, and didst rejoice: wherefore then wit thou sin against innocent blood, to slay David without cause? And Saul hearkened unto the voice of Jonathan: and Saul sware, As the Lord liveth, he shall not be slain. And Jonathan called David, and Jonathan shewed him all those things. And Jonathan brought David to Saul, and he was in his presence, as in times past. And there was war again:

and David went out, and fought with the Philistines, and slew them with a great slaughter; and they fled from him. And the evil spirit from the Lord was upon Saul, as he sat in his house with his javelin in his hand: and David played with his hand. And Saul sought to smite David ever to the wall with the javelin; but he slipped away out of Saul's presence, and he smote the javelin into the wall: and David fled, and escaped that night, Saul also sent messengers unto David's house, to watch him, and to slay him in the morning: and Michal David's wife told him, saying, if thou save not thy life to night, to morrow thou shall be slain." Can you imagine living under the type of pressure that David faced, knowing that the king you serve desires to kill you for no reason other that God's favor is upon your life? Think about how easy it would have been for David to just leave, to pack his bags and go back home and tend to his father's sheep. After all who would have blamed him, Saul would have been pleased and he would have most certainly been justified in the eyes of everyone, everyone except God that is! In God's eyes David would have failed and proven that he was not qualified for the destiny God intended for him and what is perhaps worse unwilling to pay the price for the greatness he was called to and made for. Because greatness comes with a price! What becomes evident from the story of the life of David is if he was going to lead he was going to have to encourage an army to fight when the outcome may not have appeared certain and encourage a people to follow God when the way may seem unclear. But how could God trust David to encourage an army or a nation if God could not trust David to encourage his self to stand in the face of one man. The fact of the matter is the danger and fear that David faced from Saul was minor compared to the danger and fear David would be required to face as king. So how did David have the courage to stand against the enemies of God, how do you and I have gifts that operate well enough to fulfill our destinies? God develops them in us through the trials and tests we face every day. However while God will develop them we must cultivate them, we must sow into them, pray about them, evaluate them, recognize them and surrender to them. In the 14th verse of the 18th Chapter of the 1st Book of Samuel the Bible makes a simple yet powerful statement concerning David's reaction to Saul's hatred of him when it says " And David behaved himself wisely in all his ways". In other words David did not react out of emotion, he considered the situation, he examined the events and weighted his options, he viewed where he was in light of who he was and more importantly based on who God is. How do you respond when you are in the face of adversity, when those you help turn on you, when you receive treatment you don't deserve? Do you consider where you are in light of where you are going? Do you inquire to God as to how what you are dealing with relates to what He has promised the world about you? Do you stand or do you flee? In short are you allowing your gifts to be developed?

5.

ELEMENT FIVE

The believers understanding that God intends to cultivate the believer's character so that the believer can be an effective witness for Christ.

I think it is well understood that when the 26th verse of the 1st Chapter of the Book of Genesis declared " and God said let us make man in our image, after our likeness: and let them have dominion over the fish of the sea, and over the fowl of the air, and over the cattle, and over all the earth, and over every creeping thing that creepth upon the earth" that God was not referring to the physical image of God but rather what are commonly called His communicable attributes, those characteristics of God that can be seen or experienced in the natural. It therefore stands to reason that if we are to share or demonstrate God's attributes that we must first possess them. Further, I think most would agree that Adam, prior to his fall, possessed many of the characteristics of God, but that after the fall and his subsequent separation from God Adam because less and less like God and more and more like the god of this world until virtually all of his God like Characteristics were gone, or at least buried under his flesh and carnality. However it should be equally evident from scripture that Man's degeneration did not change God's intention that man would serve as His reflection, and that God through Jesus Christ intends to restore man to his original condition and purpose.

In the 12th through 19th verses of the 5th Chapter of the Book of Romans the Apostle Paul speaking of God's plan of redemption declares "Wherefore, as by one man sin entered into the world, and death by sin; and so death passed upon all men, for that all have sinned: (for until the law sin was in the world: but sin is not imputed when there is no law. Nevertheless death reigned from Adam to Moses, even over them that had not sinned after the similitude of Adam's transgression, who is the figure of him that was to come. But not as the offense, so also is the free gift. For if through the offense of one many be dead, much more the grace of God, and the gift by grace which is by one man, Jesus Christ hath abound unto many. And not as it was by one that sinned, so is the gift: for the Judgment was by one to condemnation, but the free gift is of many offenses unto justification. For if by one man's offense death reigned by one; much more they which receive abundance of grace and of the gift of righteousness shall reign in life by one, Jesus Christ). Therefore, as by the offence of one Judgment came upon all men to condemnation; even so by the righteousness of one the free gift came upon all men unto justification to life. For as by one man's disobedience many were made sinners so by the obedience of one shall many be made righteous:" In these passages of scripture we see the beginning of God's plan for the restoration of man to His original condition and his original purpose. I believe one of the greatest errors of the modern Church is its failure to properly teach or perhaps even understand God's true plan for the redemption of man. Some in the Church believe simply that upon accepting Jesus Christ as Lord and Savior (for some simply accepting Jesus as savior will surface) God's act of redemption is complete, however, this theological position, while very popular does not line up with the weight of scripture. Those who hold this view completely ignore the truth of both progressive righteousness and progressive salvation. The Apostle Paul makes two important statements on the subject of progressive salvation (or perhaps it should be referred to as progressive transformation of the believer). The first of those statements is found in the 28th through 30th verses of the 8th Chapter of the Book of Romans. The 28th through 30the verses of the 8th Chapter of the Book of Romans provides "For whom he did foreknow, he also did predestinate to be conformed to the image of His son, that he might be the first born among many brethren. Moreover whom he did predestinate, he also called: and who he called them he also justified: and whom he justified, them he also glorified" or as the amplified states " We are assured and know that [God being a partner in their labor], all things work together and are [fitting into a plan] for good to those who love God and are called according to [his] design and purpose, For those whom he foreknew-of whom he was aware and loved beforehand-he also destined from the beginning (foreordaining them) to be molded into the image of His son [and bare inwardly his likeness], that he might become the first-born among many brethren. And those whom He thus foreordained He also called; and those whom He called He also justified-acquitted; made righteous, putting them into right standing with Himself. And those who He justified He also glorified-raising them to a heavenly dignity and condition [state of being]." As I examine these scriptures there are a few things that immediately come to mind. The first is that everything works for the good of those called by God. One of the greatest challenges to our maturity as Christians is to move beyond the need to evaluate everything that happens in our lives, our experiences in terms of their immediate impact on our souls. In the 28th verse of the 8th Chapter of the Book of Romans the Apostle Paul wrote "and we know that all things work together for the good of them that love God, to them who are called according to His purpose" it does not say that we know that all things will feel good, or seem good, or that all things that we think are good. It is important as believers to recognize that there will be times that we experience things that are contrary to our desires, that are unpleasant and even painful that work for our good. In much the same way as a cancer patient must undergo treatment that is sometime unpleasant and even painful in order for them to become healthy, so too must we sometimes undergo experiences that while unpleasant or even painful are ultimately for our good. However, far too often we allow our flesh to determine the value we will place on an event rather than the ultimate impact the event will have on our becoming more like Jesus. I can only imagine the number of times where we have complained, resisted, and even rebelled against God because God in an act of his unfailing love allowed or perhaps even caused an event to occur that while was unpleasant to us was in our best interest, especially if the event resulted in our losing something or someone. When I think about those moments when I have suffered loss from a natural perspective, (and there have been more that a few) I think about the statement that Jesus made in the 2nd verse of the 15th Chapter of the Gospel according to Saint John which reads " Every branch in me that beareth not fruit he taketh away: and every branch that bareth fruit, he purgeth" or as the amplified translation states " Any branch in me that does not bear fruit- that stops baring- he cuts away (trims off, takes away), and he cleanses and repeatedly prunes every branch that continues to bear fruit, to make it bear more and richer and more excellent fruit." I cannot emphasis enough how differently God sees our lives and the events that occur in them than we do. So often the things we complain about are the very things that are the most beneficial to us, at least from God's perspective. I think it is tragic that there are some in the Body of Christ whose teaching directly contradicts God's word on this point, there are even some in who hold leadership positions that teach those that follow them that any hardship, any loss experienced by a believer is either a result of a lack of faith or an indication of some sin for which the believer has not repented. What is truly sad about their teachings is that they have the affect of increasing the suffering that the believer experiencing the difficulty endures at a time when they need comfort the most. This in turn causes many to turn away from God and engage in what is often pointless and cruel self-examination as they search for some secret sin which is the cause of their suffering. However, the Bible clearly teaches us that our suffering is not always a result of our sin. King David spoke directly on this issue in the 19th verse of the 34th division of psalms when he declared "many are the afflictions of the righteous: but the

Lord delivereth him out of them all." In this scripture David makes it clear that afflictions or difficulties are part of the life of the righteous and not simply a consequence of sin and faithlessness. In addition, the Bible is full of example of people who experienced great hardship that were not a result of their sin or a lack faith, one such example was Job. In the 1st verse of the 1st Chapter of the Book of Job the Bible speaking of Job declares " There was a man in the land of Uz, whose name was job; and that man was perfect and upright, and one that feared God, and eschewed evil.' I find it interesting how many people attempt to find fault with Job as a means of validating their theology view that adversity is an indication of a lack of faith or un-repented sin, but however hard they try the statement the Bible makes about Job is clear that Job "was perfect and upright, one who feared God, and eschewed evil." However, I cannot think of a Biblical character who endured a greater hardship than job, (with the exception of Jesus). In fact we see exactly what God thought about Job in the 3rd verse of the 2nd Chapter of the Book of Job which provides "And the Lord said unto satan, hast thou considered my servant Job, that there is none like him in the earth, a perfect and an upright man, one that feareth God, and eschewed evil? And still be holdesth fast his integrity, although thou movest me against him, to destroy him without cause". Have you ever wonder what God says about you, about your uprightness, your hatred of evil, your integrity? Have you ever wondered if the things you have been going through were God's way of finding out who you really are deep down inside? In the 12th through 15th verses of the 3rd Chapter of 1st Book of Corinthian the Apostle Paul wrote " Now if any man build upon this foundation gold, silver, precious stones, wood, hay, stubble; every man's work shall be made manifest: for the day shall declare it, because it shall be revealed by fire; and the fire shall try every man's work of what sort it is if any man's abideth which he hath built thereupon, he shall receive a reward, if any man's work shall be burned, he shall suffer loss: but he himself shall he saved; yet so as by fire" So often we see the difficult moments of our lives a problems or punishment but what if God is allowing us to be tested because He is confident we will prevail? What if God is simply trying to perfect His character in you? In the 3rd through 5th verses of the 5th Chapter of the Book of Romans the Apostle Paul wrote "And not only so, but we glory in tribulation also: knowing that tribulation worketh patience and patience, experience; and experience hope: and hope maketh not ashamed; because the love of God is shed abroad in our hearts by the Holy Ghost which is given unto us" perhaps this is why Apostle Paul states in this 28th verse of the 8th the Chapter "and we know that all things work together for good to them that love God, to them who are the called according to his purpose." As I read this passage it becomes clear that the pivotal issue here is our love for God. If we truly love God then we will desire God's will to be fulfilled in and through us because it will make us more like Jesus and how we respond to our suffering will speak volumes concerning the place He truly holds in our hearts because the more we love him the more we will be willing to endure hardship to please and honor Him. The Book Daniel contains the account of Shadrach, Meshach and Abednego and their trial at the hands of Nebuchadnezzar because of their refusal to worship his gods. In the 16th through 18th verses of the 3rd Chapter of the Book of Daniel the Bible records Shadrach, Meshach and Abednego's response to Nebuchadnezzar's demand that they worship his gods and provides "Shadrach, Meshach and Aded-nego answered and said to the king, O

Nebuchadnezzar we are not careful to answer thee in this matter, if it be so, our God whom we serve is able to deliver us from the burning fiery furnace, and he will deliver us out of thine hands, O king. But if not, be it known unto thee, O king that we will not serve thy gods, nor worship the golden image which thou has set up." What a message their statement made about their devotion to God. Not only did they affirm their belief that God was able to save them, but in addition (and I believe more importantly) that if God choose not to save them they would rather suffer a painful death than dishonor Him through worship of Nebuchadnezzar's gods. How often do you hear of such devotion to God today. Just think what the Body of Christ could do to change the world if more Christians had the type of devotion that these three boys had. When I think about this story I am amazed at the timing of God. How He would step in right after they demonstrated their commitment to Him, in other words the moment they past the test. But what is even more amazing to me is how this is the same test that you and I face, will we be willing to suffer loss in order to honor our God. It may not be a test as dramatic as the threat of being thrown in a literal furnace but that doesn't mean that the tests we face are not as real or that our response is any less important. Each of us will experience tests and trials in our lives that may tempt us to turn our back on God or compromise the principles of His word. In those moments it is important that we recognize that while we may not enjoy the experience or even understand why we have to endure it, it will work for our good and the good of those around us.

In addition, in the 29th verse of the 8th Chapter of the Book of Romans the Bible provides " for whom he did foreknow, he also did predestinate to be conformed to the image of His son, that He might be the first born among many brethren" again clearly establishing God's intent that we serve as His representatives. In this scripture the Apostle Paul provides clear insight into the mind of God as it relates to His intentions towards man. In this verse of scripture the Apostle Paul makes it clear that God's intention is to conform us to the image of Christ was not merely a reaction to man's current condition, but rather part of God's original plan. When I consider how purposeful God is and how every action, and every step in God's plan has been carefully laid out before man's creation I find myself in awe. Have you ever really, I mean really considered the fact that God put a plan in place to redeem and restore man not only before the fall of man into sin, but before man was created. I find great comfort in the knowledge that not only does God know the mistakes that we as his children make, but that God has arranged it so that they will work for our ultimate good. Through out scripture God has spoken to man about the need for man to be conformed or changed so that man represents the image and likeness of God. One of the most well know examples of which is found in the 1st and 2nd verses of the 12th Chapter of the Book of Romans where the Apostle Paul writing to the Church of Rome admonished them by saying "I beseech you therefore brethren, by the mercies of God, that ye present your bodies as a living sacrifice holy, acceptable to God, which is your reasonable service, And be not conformed to this world: but be ye transformed by the renewing of your mind, that ye may prove what is the good, and acceptable and perfect will of God" As I read this scripture what I find so interesting is the formula, if you will, that God establishes for our transformation, step 1) present your bodies to God; step 2) do nor be conformed to this world; and step 3) be ye transformed by the renewing of your mind. These three steps create an even clearer picture of our transformation when viewed through the eyes of the Amplified translation which reads "I appeal to you therefore, brethren, and beg of you in view of [all] the mercies of God, to make a decisive dedication of your bodies [presenting all your members and faculties] as a living sacrifice, holy (devoted, consecrated) and well pleasing to God, which is your reasonable (rational, intelligent) services and spiritual worship. Do not be conformed to this world (this age), [fashioned after and adapted to its external, superficial customs], but be transformed (changed) by the [entire] renewal of your mind [by its new ideals and its new attitudes], so that you may prove [for yourselves] what is the good and acceptable and perfect will of God, even the thing which is good and acceptable and perfect [in his sight for you]." So then step 1) to make a decisive dedication of your bodies [presenting all your members and faculties]; step 2) Do not be conformed to this world (this age), [fashioned after and adapted to its external, superficial customs], and step 3) but be transformed (changed) by the [entire] renewal of your mind [by its new ideals and its new attitudes], can you see the impact these steps would have on the life of a believer. As I write these steps my mind turns to what the Bible declares in the 7th verse of the 23rd Chapter of the Book of Proverbs which provides "For as a man thinkest in his heart, so is he" and raises a serious question that all of us who strive to live for God must address. How can we consume all of the carnal, sinful, and morally debase information which comes from our culture and hope to become transformed much less remain in the image of God? I believe that the obvious answer is that we can't,

We can't consume all the carnality of this world and make a decisive dedications of our bodies, all our members and faculties to God, we can't consume all the carnality of this world and not be shaped or fashioned by its external superficial customs, we can't consume all the carnality of this world and renew our minds by adopting new ideals and new attitudes, we can't. I firmly believe that the Body of Christ's acceptance of all the world has to offer is resulting in our becoming salt without seasoning and a candle without light. Further, when we examine the Book of acts and the writings of the early Church and read about how the power of God moved so freely and so consistently you cannot help but wonder how great a role the social isolation of the early Church played in the power of God being experienced and by extension how much we have lost by virtue of our acceptance and involvement in the larger society. Moreover, I believe that each of us must consider what value we place on social acceptance as well as the price we are willing to pay because the Bibles warning about the dangers of worldliness are very clear. One such warning is found in the admonishment of the Apostle Paul in the 2nd verse of the 12th Chapter of the Book of Romans when he instructed the Church at Rome and be not conformed to this world" however, I believe a clearer understanding of the warning is provided in the amplified translation which provides "do not be conformed to this world-this age, fashioned after and adapted to its external, superficial customs." Another such admonishment is found in the 15th and 16th verses of the 2nd Chapter of the 1st Epistle of John which provides "love not the world, neither the things that are in the world. If any man loves this world, the love of the father is not in him. For all that is in the world, the lust of the flesh, and the lust of the eyes, and the pride of life is not of the father, but is of this world or as the amplified translates states "Do not love or cherish the world or the things that are in the world. If anyone loves the world, love for the father is not in him. For all that is in the world-the lust of the flesh[cravings for sensual gratification] and the lust of the eyes [greedy longings of the mind] and the pride of life[assurance in one's own resources or in the stability of earthly things]- these do not come from the father but are from the world[itself]" Both of these scriptures make it abundantly clear that those of us who are members of the Body of Christ should not be shaped by or have our affections on the things of this world. However what is perhaps the clearest Admonishment against being conformed to the image of this world came from our Lord Jesus Christ himself. In the 24th verse of the 6th Chapter of the Gospel according to Saint Matthew Jesus while teaching His disciples on Christian ethics declared " No man can serve two masters: for either he will hate the one, and love the other; or else he will hold to the one, and despise the other. Ye cannot serve God and mammon" and there is at least an implicit statement in the 1st and 2nd verses of the 12th Chapter of the Book of Romans that we must choose, whether we will be conformed to the image of this world and serve mammon or be transformed by the renewing of our minds and serve God. But choose we must! We must choose whether we will be shaped and defined by the things of the flesh or by the things of God. As I write this I realize that there are some in the body of Christ that may not have a clear understanding of the choice they are required to make and are not confident in their ability to properly distinguish between the two. For those who may find themselves in this situation I would invite you to examine the 19th through 23rd verses of the 5th Chapter of the Book of Galatians where the Apostle Paul writes " Now the works of the flesh are manifest, which are these; adultery, fornication, uncleanness, lasciviousness, idolatry, witchcraft, hatred, variance, emulations, wrath, strife, seditions, heresies, envying, murder, drunkenness, revellings and the like such like: of the which I tell you before, as I have also told you in the past, that they which do such things shall not inherit the kingdom of God. But the fruit of the spirit is love, joy, peace, longsuffering, gentleness, goodness, faith, meekness, temperance: and against such there is not law" drawing a clear distinction between the things of this world and the things of God. In examining those things that the Apostle Paul classifies as the works of the flesh it is important that we look beyond the items contained on the list to ensure we not only gain an understanding of the things contained on the list but also the behaviors they produce. If we were to examine the society and culture in which we live, regardless of where on the planet you may find yourself and the value system they produce we will discover that the works of the flesh are the characteristics upon which the world's value system is based. When we talk about the ills of the modern society we often focus on the impact that rapid and blatant sexuality plays in the destruction of our value system, however the worlds obsession with sexual gratification is only one of the issues that we must guard against and each of the works of the flesh mentioned by the Apostle Paul produces a host of issues that threaten to not only overwhelm us but also result in our being conformed to a world that is contrary to God's will and hinder our transformation into the image of God. So what do we do, how do we resist the endless stream of carnal information which has as it affect if not its design our being conformed into the image of a world that God despises? The short answer is we fight!

In the 3rd through 6th verses of the 10th chapter of the 2nd Book of Corinthians the Apostle Paul provides us with vital information on how to fight against the forces of this world that seek to conform us when he wrote " For though we walk in the flesh, we do not war after the flesh: for the weapons of our warfare are not carnal, but mighty through God to the pulling down of strongholds; casting down imaginations, and every high thing that exalteth itself against the knowledge of Christ; and having in a readiness to revenge all disobedience, when your obedience is fulfilled" or as the amplified translation states "For though we walk [live] in the flesh, we are not carrying on our warfare according to the flesh and using mere human weapons: For the weapons of our warfare are not physical (weapons of flesh and blood), but they are mighty before God for the overthrowing and destruction of strongholds, [in as much as we] refute arguments and theories and reasonings and every proud and lofty thing that sets itself up against the (true) knowledge; and we lead every thought and purpose away captive into the obedience of Christ, the Messiah, the anointed on, being in readiness to punish every [insubordinate for his] disobedience, when your own submission and obedience [as a Church] are fully secured and complete."

In this scripture we see that this battle is not fought in the natural but in the spiritual because it is not a battle for the control of our bodies but rather for our souls. It is not a battle over our behavior it is a battle over our values and our beliefs, it is a battle of the thought processes and priorities that determine what we think is possible, required, important and valuable. It is a battle over who we think we are and what we think makes us important, it is a battle of our identity and our destinies. The weapons we use in this warfare are mighty through God, not through ourselves, because there is no amount of commitment, will power, personal righteousness, or even fear that will, absent the power of God, have any success in this battle. It is only the power of God that can save us. When we receive the gift of salvation there is a deposit of the Holy Spirit that enters us which serves as our assurance of the fullness to come. Once deposited in us He begins to demonstrate what is acceptable to Him. One of the clearest examples of the workings of the Holy Spirit in the life of a believer is found in the 1st through 11th verses of the 43rd chapter of the book of Ezekiel where the prophet Ezekiel wrote "Afterwards he brought me to the gate, even the gate that looketh towards the east: and, Behold, the glory of the God of Israel came from the way of the east: And his voice was like a noise of many waters: and the earth shinned with his glory. And it was according to the appearance of the vision that I saw when I came to destroy the city: And the visions were like the visions that I saw by the river Chebar; and I fell upon my face and the glory of the Lord came into the house by the way of the gate whose prospect is towards the east. So the spirit took me up, and brought me into the inner court; and, behold, the glory of the Lord filled the house. And I heard him speaking unto me out of the house; and the man stood by me. And he said unto me, son of man, the place of my throne, and the place of the soles of my feet, where I will dwell in the midst of the Children of Israel for ever, and my Holy name, shall the house of Israel no more defile, neither they, not their kings, by their whoredom, nor by the carcasses of their kings in their high places, in their setting of their threshold by my thresholds. And their posts by my posts, and the wall between me and then, they have even defiled my Holy name by their abominations that they have in mine anger. Now let them put away their whoredom, and the carcasses of their Kings, far from me, and I will dwell in the midst of them for ever. Thou son of man, shew the house to the house of Israel, that they may be ashamed of their iniquities: and let them measure the pattern. And if they be ashamed of all that thy have done, shew them the form of the house, and the fashion thereof, and the goings out thereof, and the comings in thereof, and all forms thereof and all the ordinances thereof, and all the forms thereof, and all the laws thereof: and write it in their sight, that they may keep the whole form thereof, and all the ordinances thereof, and do them" In this scripture we see some of the most amazing things. As we begin our examination of this text we must understanding that this scripture discussed a temple that has never actually been construction in the natural but rather uses the temple as a type and shadow of the body of Christ collectively and each of use individually and in this regard paints a vivid picture of each of us in our role as the dwelling place of God and reminds us of the Apostle Paul's Admonishment towards personal righteousness contained in the 18th through 20th verses of the 6th Chapter of the 1st Book of Corinthians which reads " Flee fornication every sin that a man doeth is without the body; but he that committeth fornication sinneth against his own body. What? Know ye not that your body is the temple of the Holy Ghost which is in you, which ye have of God, and ye are not your own? For ye are brought with a price: therefore glorify God in your body, and in your spirit, which are God's" Which not only reminds us that we are the dwelling place of God but also that as His dwelling place we must be spiritually clean and fit for His inhabitation. That is the process which is discussed in the 1st through 11th verses of the 43 Chapter of the Book of Ezekiel. In these passages of scripture we see the glory of God, the God of Israel, which is the Spirit of

God enter into the temple from the way of the east, which is a representation that the Holy Spirit enters in through Christ and only through Christ. The image of the Holy Spirit entering through Christ reminds us that Jesus' sacrificial act on the cross is our only means of access to God and the only prerequisite to receiving the gift of the Holy Spirit. However, it must be clearly understood that the acceptance of Jesus as Lord and savior is the beginning of a process of spiritual purification and maturity. Once we receive the gift of the Holy Spirit our spiritual eyes begin to open as we begin to see the fuller truth about Jesus, about the world we live in and most importantly ourselves. This fact is underscored by the description of the earth shinning with His glory. This point cannot be emphasized enough because far too often there are those who have never received the gift of the Holy Spirit but are attempting to lead people into the light and they have not been brought out of the darkness themselves. These are the people Jesus referred to in the 10th through 14th verses of the 15th Chapter of the Gospel according to Saint Matthew which reads "And he called the multitude, and said unto them, hear and understand: not that which goeth into the mouth defileth a man; but that which cometh out of the mouth, this defileth a man, Then came His disciples, and said unto Him, knoweth thou that the Pharisees were offended, after thy heard this saying? But He answered and said every plant, which my heavenly father has not planted, shall be rooted up, Let them alone: they are the blind leaders of the blind. And if the blind lead the blind both shall fall into the ditch." Not having the spirit of God in them yet attempting to discern spiritual things. It is only when the light of God's glory is seen can the truth be revealed. As the glory of God is shined in the temple the true condition of the temple is revealed just as the light of

Christ reveals the truth of what lies deep with in us. The challenge we face is how we respond to what is revealed. Most of us believe that we are good people, with kind hearts and good intentions and feel not only comfortable but justified in our beliefs and are quite content with how we are compared to our friends, family, co-workers and our communities. In fact some of us feel confident that we are in a morally if not spiritually superior position compared to those around us and most certainly compared to those we see on television and read about in the news. In point of fact I truly believe that the reason for the popularity of much what is produced by the entertainment industry is based in its ability to produce images of humanity that are so tragic and so debased that they reinforce our sense of moral superiority. However, the question is not how you or I compare to the characters on the most popular television shows or movies, it is not how our lives line up next to those individuals whose lives and circumstances are sufficiently tragic that they land in the news, it is not even how we are doing compared to our friends, family, co-workers, neighbors or even our fellow church members it is solely and simply how we are doing in the eyes of God when the light of His glory is shined deep within us, that part of us that no one sees but God. Listen to what the Spirit of God had to say about the condition of the human soul in the 7th and 8th verses of the 43 Chapter of the Book of Ezekiel which provides "And he said unto me, son of man, the place of my throne, and the place of the soles of my feet, where I will dwell in the midst of the Children of Israel for ever, no more defile, neither they, nor their kings, by their whoredom, nor by the caracaras of their kings in their high places. In their settings of their thresholds by my thresholds, and their posts by my posts, and the wall between, me and them, they have even defiled my Holy name by their abominations that they have committed: wherefore, I have consumed them in my anger." In these passages of scripture God is revealing His view of the soul who has been conformed to the image of this world, The soul that finds its authority from sources (their kings) other than Him, those sources who are living and those (carcasses) who have died but still assert authority over us. As I think about this I am horrified at how members of the body of Christ have based the operation of their daily lives on principles that are contrary to the word of God and look to people for counsel who are not saved. In addition, when the spirit of God speaks of whoredom in the 7th verse He is speaking about what we commit our affections and allegiances to, what we value and what we worship, in short He is talking about idolatry. Many of us in the modern Church have loss sight of the issue of idolatry because we do not understand idolatry is a question of what or who we recognize as our source, our source of peace, our source of prosperity, our source of importance, our source of health, of love, of fulfillment, of protection, of identity, of acceptance and when we acknowledged a source of these things as well as others we are raising up an idol above God. Furthermore, when the spirit of God speaks of thresholds He is speaking of the standards we raise up in place of His. The truly unfortunate part is that we do not understand how pervasive this problem is in the body of Christ, when you define success, do you think of having a good job, a nice house in a good neighborhood, a nice car, and perhaps a comfortable amount of money in the bank, the acceptance of your peers or community. If you are like most you do. But where did that picture of success come from, was it taught by Jesus or does it come from the world to which we are admonished not to conform? Perhaps a more important question is how does what you do to obtain it and maintain it line up with the word of God, how does God view the choices we make and the life we lead? In the 15th verse of the 16th Chapter of the Gospel according to Saint Luke Jesus warns us of the danger of living a life based on the world's standards when the Bible speaking of Jesus provides " And He said unto them, Ye are they which justify yourselves before men; but God knoweth your hearts: For that which is highly esteemed among men is an abomination in the sight of God" and this is exactly the condition that the Apostle Paul warned the Church of Roman about when he admonished them in the 1st and 2nd verses of the 12th Chapter of the Book of Romans not to be conformed to this world but be transformed by the renewing of their minds. Further it is the process of transformation that the Spirit of Lord is addressing in the 9th through 11th verses of the 43rd Chapter of the Book of Ezekiel where He commanded the Prophet Ezekiel "Now let them put away their whoredom and the carcasses of their kings, far from me, and I will dwell in the midst of them for ever. Thou son of Man, shew the house to the house of Israel, that they may be ashamed of their iniquities: and let them measure the pattern and if they be ashamed of all that they have done, shew them the form of the house, and the fashion thereof, and the goings out thereof, and the comings in thereof, and all the forms thereof, and all the ordinances thereof, and all the forms thereof, and all the laws thereof: and write it in their sight, that they may keep the whole form thereof, and all the ordinances thereof, and to do them." At this point there are a couple of points I want to make clear. The first is that the pattern and every ordinance points to Jesus and Jesus alone, this is not a call to tradition or ritual, but it is a call to order, it is a call for transformation into the image of

Jesus. In the 28th and 29th verses of the 8th Chapter of the Book of Romans the Apostle Paul addresses this point when he declares "And we know that all things work together for good to them that love God, to them who are the called according to His purpose. For whom he did foreknow, he also did predestinate to be conformed to the image of His son, that he might be the first born of among many brethren" as we move about in our daily lives it is important to recognize that everything that transpired is used to transform us into the image of Jesus which is God's ultimate purpose for not only our salvation but our lives. Many times we are faced with confusing and difficult situations which challenge us to our very core and we find ourselves asking God why. In those moments I think it is helpful to remember that all of those events while tragic will be used to help us be transformed into the image of Jesus. The Final point I want to make is that our transformation into the image of Jesus is both our assignment and our choice. In the 9th and 11th verses of the 43rd Chapter of the Book of Ezekiel the Spirit of the Lord spoke and said " Now let them put away their whoredom, and the carcasses of their kings, far from me, and I will dwell in the midst of them forever.. and If they be ashamed of all that they have done, shew then the form of the house, and the fashion thereof, and the goings out thereof, and the comings in thereof, and the coming in thereof, and all the forms thereof, and all the laws thereof: and write it in their sight, that they may keep the whole from thereof, and the ordinances thereof, and do them." In these passages of scripture God placed the responsibility for the transformation of our soul on each of us. This fact is one of the basis of our personal relationships with Jesus Christ, It is interesting to me how many in the Body of Christ have placed the development of their walk with God and the development of their Christian Character solely in the hands of others and have assumed no personal responsibility for becoming who God has ordained them to be. There are many of who find themselves going from church to church conference to conference, prophet to prophet looking for a word or an encounter that will do for them what only their personal desire and commitment will do. Never coming to the understanding that the road of transformation is a journey that each of us must take for ourselves, The Apostle Paul spoke directly to this issue in the 12th and 15th verses of the 2nd Chapter of the Book of Philippians when he wrote "wherefore, my beloved, as ye have always obeyed, not as in my presence only, but now much more in my absence, work out your own salvation with fear and trembling, for it is God which worketh in you both to will and to do of His good pleasure. Do all things without murmuring and disputing: that ye may be blameless and harmless, the sons of God, without rebuke in the midst of a crooked and perverse nation, among whom ye shine as lights in the world" The light that the Apostle Paul is referring to is the character of Jesus that God expects you and I to develop in ourselves, that character that your are maturing in as a son of God.

6.

ELEMENT SIX

The Believers understanding that process prolongs process and process always proceeds prosperity:

Much of the last chapter centered around the declaration that the Apostle Paul wrote in the 28th and 29th verses of the 8th Chapter of the Book of Romans which provides "and we know that all things work together for good to them that love God, to them who are the called according to his purpose. For whom he did foreknow, he also did predestinate to be conformed to the image of his son that he might be the first born of many brethren". Which assures us that every thing that we encounter or experience is used by God as part of our process, I realize that for some in the body of Christ "process" is both an unpleasant and unfamiliar term that is in direct conflict with the modern Church's name it and claim it theology, which suggests that our relationship with God is solely or at least primarily about our receipt of our "promise" which is a fulfilled, happy life. However despite what this theology suggests the importance of our successful completion of our process is taught through out the Bible both in the old and new testaments and not only is an understanding of its importance vital, it is unavoidable. One such example is found in the 29th chapter of the Book of Jeremiah. In the 29th chapter of the Book of Jeremiah, the prophet Jeremiah writes to the nation of Israel living in Babylonian captivity concerning God's instructions for their conduct while in captivity as well as the circumstances under which they will be delivered. I believe that the 29th Chapter of the Book of Jeremiah, like much if not all of the old testament serves as a metaphor of the life of the members of the

Body of Christ and therefore provides us with valuable insight into the ways and activities of God and further, should help establish our expectations concerning both our natural and spiritual realities. In the 9th through 14th verses of the 29th Chapter of the Book of Jeremiah, the Prophet Jeremiah declared " Thus said the Lord of hosts, the God of Israel, unto all that are carried away captives, whom I have caused to be carried away from Jerusalem unto Babylon; build ye houses, and dwell in them; and plant gardens, and eat the fruit of them; take ye wives, and beget sons and give your daughters to husbands, that they may bear sons and daughters; that they may be increased there, and not diminished. And seek the peace of the city whither I have caused you to be carried away captives, and pray unto the Lord for it: for in the peace thereof shall ye have peace. For this saith the Lord of hosts, the God of Israel; let not your prophets and your diviners, that be in the midst of you deceive you, neither hearken to your dreams which ye cause to be dreamed. For they prophesy falsely unto you in my name: I have not sent them, saith the Lord. For thus saith the Lord, that after seventy years be accomplished at Babylon I will visit you, and perform my good word towards you, in causing you to return to this place. For I know the thoughts that I think towards you, saith the Lord, thoughts of peace, and not evil, to give you an expected end. Then shall Ye call upon me, and ye shall go and pray unto me, and I will hearken unto you. And ye shall seek me, and find me, when ye shall search for me with all your heart, And I will be found of you, saith the Lord: and I will turn away your captivity, and I will gather you from all the nations and places whither I have driven you, saith the Lord; and I will bring you again into the place whence I caused you to be carried away captive." In these passages of scripture there a number of key points that need to be addressed. The first point that needs to be addressed is that the condition they found themselves in was caused by God. In the 4th verse of the 29th Chapter of the Book of Jeremiah the Bible provides "thus saith the Lord of host, the God of Israel, unto all that are carried away captives, whom I have caused to be carried away from Jerusalem unto Babylon." When ever we, like the nation of Israel, find ourselves in an difficult or unpleasant situation our natural response is to assume that we are under attack and indentify an enemy, (whether real or imagined) to blame. In point of fact in the modern Church we spend so much of our time and focus on blaming satan that we have elevated him from the fallen broken powerless foe that he is to the status of an all present menacing foe who has knowledge and power that rivals that of God himself. However, the truth is satan has no power in the life of a believer and can only operate through the influence we chose to give him, he is not a threat to anyone who chooses not to listen to him and has no power to thwart the will of God in the believer's life. The truth is that satan can do no more to any of us than God will allow. This point is made clear to us in the 6th through 12th verses of the 1st chapter of the Book of Job which provides "Now there was a day when the sons of God came to present themselves before God the Lord, and satan came also among them. And the Lord said to satan whence cometh thou? Then satan answered the Lord, and said, from going to and fro in the earth, and from walking up and down in it. And the Lord said unto satan, hast thou considered my servant job, that there is none like him in the earth, a perfect man and upright man, one that feareth God, and escheweth evil? Then satan answered the Lord, and said, doth Job fear God for nought? Hast not thou made a hedge about him, and about his house and about all that he hath on every side? Thou hast blessed the work of his hands, and his substance is increased in the land. But put forth thine hand now, and touch all that he hath, and he will curse thee to thy face. And the Lord said unto satan behold, all that he hath is in thy power; only upon himself put not forth thine hand. So satan went forth from the presence of the Lord." In this scripture the Bible makes it clear that satan does not have full reign to do his will unrestrained but can only operate in the areas of our lives where he is permitted by God and therefore serves, unwittingly as an agent of God's will. When ever I think about the truth of satan's efforts to hinder and harm the Body of Christ I think of the statement that Joseph made in to his brothers in the 20th verse of the 50th Chapter of the Book of Genesis which reads "But as for you, ye thought evil against me; but God meant it unto good, to bring to pass, as it is this day, to save much people alive." As well as what the Apostle Paul wrote in the 28th verse of the 8th Chapter of the Book of Romans which provides "And we know that all things work together for good to them that love God, to them who are called according to his purpose." Just as it was with the Nation of Israel in the 29th Chapter of the Book of Jeremiah so it is with the Body of Christ today, God uses those who would do us evil to promote our good by provoking them to take actions or engage in conduct that while often not pleasing to us, places us in a place of process so that through that process many people may live. This brings me to my next point, that their condition was designed to remove things from them that displeased God. Theirs was idolatry, what is yours, what is the thing that you have given yourself to that is contrary to your very purpose? Many of us have no idea what may be in us that opposes God's very purpose for our lives and as a result find ourselves protesting the very process that is necessary to cause us to prosper. When I speak of prospering I am not talking about our definition of prospering, with its focus on comfort and materialism, I am talking about prospering based on God's definition, the fulfillment of the destiny for which you and I were created. For the Nation of Israel it was to be a chosen people, a people set apart for God, living their lives based on the laws, customs and precepts established by God and given to them by God through their God ordained leaders, those men who He set aside (consecration) for His own use. This was their purpose, their destiny to be the greatest, most successful most prosperous nation on the face of the earth. To serve as the candle on the hill that shined with God's glory, so that the nations who did not know God, would see them and witness what it was to live in God's favor, His mercy, His goodness, His generosity, His protection and desire and seek God for themselves. The only question is how could they do that if they had begun to worship other gods, the gods of their neighbors and those around them, for that matter how can we? How can we teach those who do not know Christ to love Christ exclusively when we love so many other things, can those who are adulterous teach faithfulness so others, can we truly teach that Christ is the only way while we are trying to many other ways ourselves? These are the questions that the Body of Christ must begin to ask ourselves, Lets take a look at what God, through the prophet Jeremiah spoke to the Nation of Israel concerning their captivity in the 1st through 13th verses of the 25th Chapter of the Book of Jeremiah where the Bible provides " The word that came to Jeremiah concerning all the people of Judah in the fourth year of Jehoiakin the son of Josiah king of Judah, that was the first year of Nebuchadnezzar king of Babylon; the which Jeremiah the prophet spake unto all the people of Judah, and to all the inhabitants of Jerusalem, saying, from the thirteenth year of Josiah the son of Amon king of Judah, even unto this day, that is the three twentieth year, the word of the Lord hath come unto me, and I have spoken unto you, rising early and speaking; but ye have not harkened. And the Lord hath sent unto you all his servants the prophets, rising early and sending them; but ye have not harkened, nor inclined your ear to hear. They said, turn ye again now every one from his evil way, and from the evil of your doings, and dwell in the land that the Lord hath given unto you and your fathers forever and ever: And go not after other gods to serve them, and to worship them, and provoke me not to anger with the works of your hands; and I will do you no hurt, Yet ye have not harkened unto me, saith the Lord; that ye might provoke me to anger with the works of your hands to your own hurt. Therefore, thus saith the Lord of hosts; because ye have not heard my words, behold I will send and take all the families of the north, saith the Lord, and Nebuchadnezzar the king of Babylon, my servant, and will bring them against this land, and against the inhabitants thereof, and against all these nations round about, and will utterly destroy them, and make them an astonishment and an hissing, and perpetual desolation, Moreover, I will take from them the voice of mirth, and the voice of gladness, the voice of the bridegroom and the voice of the bride, the sound of the millstones, and the light of the candles. And this whole land shall be a desolation, and an astonishment; and these nations shall serve the kings of Babylon seventy years. And it shall come to pass, when seventy years are accomplished, that I will punish the king of Babylon, and that nation, saith the Lord, for their iniquity, and the land of the Chaldeans, and will make it perpetual desolations. And I will bring upon that land all my words which I have pronounced against it, even all that is written in this book, which Jeremiah hath prophesied against all the nations" as I read these passages of scripture I cannot help but think how much the fate of Nebuchadnezzar and the nation of Babylon is similar to the fate of satan and all those in his kingdom. Those, who allow themselves to be used for evil against the people of God to change the heart and behavior of those God loves, and find themselves awaiting destruction, as those God loves move deeper and deeper into their destiny. If we were to examine the story of the Nation of Israel's experience in Egypt we would discover a very similar pattern. The Nation of Israel having to come to enjoy the favor of the Egyptians and having loss sight both of their destiny as a Nation unto God, and that the purpose of God moving them into Egypt was to ensure their survival during a seven year famine suddenly find themselves living under the ruler ship of a king who did not remember the favor that they enjoyed because of Joseph. In the 7th through 14th verses of the 1st Chapter of the Book of Exodus the Bible records the Nation of Israel's change of circumstances from blessed to bondage under Egyptian rule when it provides "And the Children of Israel were fruitful, and increased abundantly, and multiplied, and waxed exceedingly mighty; and the land was filled with them. Now there arose up a new king over Egypt, which knew not Joseph. And he said unto his people, behold, the people of the Children of Israel are more and mightier that we" Come on, let us deal wisely with them; lest they muitlply, and it come to pass, that, when there falleth out any war, they join also unto our enemies, and fight against us, and so get them up out of the land, Therefore, they did set over them taskmasters to afflict them with their burdens. And they built for Pharaoh treasuries cites, Pithon and Raames But the more they afflicted them, the more they multiplied and grew. And they were grieved because of the Children of Israel, And the Egyptians made the Children of Israel to serve them with rigor: and they made their lives bitter with hard bondage, in mortar, and I brick, and in all manner of service in the field: All their service, wherein they made them serve, was with rigor." The Bible further provides that as was the case of Nebuchadnezzar and the Nation of Babylon, Pharaoh and the Egyptians faced destruction at the hands of God as God determined to deliver the Nation of Israel. In the 4th through 28th verses of the 14th Chapter of the Book of Exodus the Bible speaking of the destruction of the Egyptians Provides "And I will harden Pharaoh's heart, that he shall follow after them; and I will be honoured upon Pharaoh, and upon all his host; that the Egyptians may know that I am the LORD. And they did so. And it was told the king of Egypt that the people fled: and the heart of Pharaoh and of his servants was turned against the people, and they said, why have we done this, that we have let Israel go from serving us? And he made ready his chariot, and took his people with him: And he took six hundred chosen chariots, and all the chariots of Egypt, and captains over every one of them. And the LORD hardened the heart of Pharaoh king of Egypt, and he pursued after the children of Israel: and the children of Israel went out with an high hand. But the Egyptians pursued after them, all the horses and chariots of Pharaoh, and his horsemen, and his army, and overtook them encamping by the sea, beside Pihahiroth, before Baalzephon. And when Pharaoh drew nigh, the children of Israel lifted up their eyes, and, behold, the Egyptians marched after them; and they were sore afraid: and the children of Israel cried out unto the LORD. And they said unto Moses, because there were no graves in Egypt, hast thou taken us away to die in the wilderness? Wherefore hast thou dealt thus with us, to carry us forth out of Egypt? Is not this the word that we did tell thee in Egypt, saying, Let us alone, that we may serve the Egyptians? For it had been better for us to serve the Egyptians, than that we should die in the wilderness. And Moses said unto the people, Fear ye not, stand still, and see the salvation of the LORD, which he will shew to you today: for the Egyptians whom ye have seen to day, ye shall see them again no more for ever. The LORD shall fight for you, and ye shall hold your peace. And the LORD said unto Moses, Wherefore criest thou unto me? speak unto the children of Israel, that they go forward: But lift thou up thy rod, and stretch out thine hand over the sea, and divide it: and the children of Israel shall go on dry ground through the midst of the sea. And I, behold, I will harden the hearts of the Egyptians, and they shall follow them: and I will get my honour upon Pharaoh, and upon all his host, upon his chariots, and upon his horsemen. And the Egyptians shall know that I am the LORD, when I have gotten my honour upon Pharaoh, upon his chariots, and upon his horsemen. And the angel of God, which went before the camp of Israel, removed and went behind them; and the pillar of the cloud went from before their face, and stood behind them: And it came between the camp of the Egyptians and the camp of Israel; and it was a cloud and darkness to them, but it gave light by night to these: so that the one came not near the other all the night. And Moses stretched out his hand over the sea; and the LORD caused the sea to go back by a strong east wind all that night, and made the sea dry land, and the waters were divided. And the children of Israel went into the midst of the sea upon the dry ground: and the waters were a wall unto them on their right hand, and on their left. And the Egyptians pursued, and went in after them to the midst of the sea, even all Pharaoh's horses, his chariots, and his horsemen. And it came to pass, that in the morning watch the LORD looked unto the host of the Egyptians through the pillar of fire and of the cloud, and troubled the host of the Egyptians, And took off their chariot wheels, that they drave them heavily: so that the Egyptians said, Let us flee from the face of Israel; for the LORD fighteth for them against the Egyptians. And the LORD said unto Moses, Stretch out thine hand over the sea, that the waters may come again upon the Egyptians, upon their chariots, and upon their horsemen. And Moses stretched forth his hand over the sea, and the sea returned to his strength when the morning appeared; and the Egyptians fled against it; and the LORD overthrew the Egyptians in the midst of the sea. And the waters returned, and covered the chariots, and the horsemen, and all the host of Pharaoh that came into the sea after them; there remained not so much as one of them." In both these instances the Bible demonstrates the fate that awaits those who cause hardship upon the lives of those chosen by God, even when God places His chosen in their hands. However there is a more important point to be made by these two examples. In each of these examples as well as countless others in the Old Testament and perhaps even more in our lives today there is a pattern that emerges, that I believe is important for us to understand. In each instance we see the Nation of Israel in the case of the examples in the Old Testament and many of us in the case of the Body of Christ having been ordained by God, to live a life that is not only pleasing to Him but one that is directed by Him. A life that by virtue of its very existence draws a stark and undeniable contrast between us and those who do not know God, not only by our behavior and the values upon which our behavior is based but our understanding of who we are and who we serve. This contrast is not only the defining purpose of our lives but is the very purpose for our lives, it is the reason for our blessings, our protection and even the instructions given to us by God concerning how to live our lives. It is the very thing that allows our lives to give God glory. However in order for this contract to exist we must be willing to live our lives in a manner that is distinct from those people who live in the world. We must love God more than the things of the world and desire to please Him more than we desire to please ourselves. But perhaps more importantly than that we must trust God and look to God as our source of everything. It is in this area that the Nation of Israel failed both in terms of their remaining in Egypt longer than the seven years required to survive the famine and in terms of the Nation of Israel looking to the false gods of their neighbors in the period which proceeded their Babylonian captivity. This is what the Bible describes as idolatry and in both cases resulted in the Nation of Israel living in iniquity. Despite God's promises which were handed down from generation to generation, despite God's repeated demonstrations of His power and His willingness to provide for and protect them, the Nation of Israel continued to place their trust in the physical god's of man's creation instead of the God who created them. But are we any different, behind our finely tuned religious serves, our nice Spiritual clichés, our assertion of being Kingdom minded people does our heart, our devotion, out faith really belong to God or do they belong to the god's of this world. In the 10th through 14th verses of the 29th Chapter of the Book of Jeremiah the Bible declares "For thus saith the Lord, that after seventy years be accomplished at Babylon I will visit you, and perform my good word towards you, in causing you to return to this place. For I know the thoughts that I think towards you, saith the Lord, thoughts of peace, and not of evil, to give you an expected end. Then shall ye call upon me, and ye shall go and pray unto me, and I will hearken unto you. And ye shall seek me, and find me when ye shall search for me with all your heart. And I will be found of you, saith the Lord: and I will turn away your captivity, and I will gather you from all the nations, and from all the places whether I have driven you, saith the Lord; and I will bring you again into the place whence I caused you to be carried away captive." In examining this scripture it becomes clear that the process that God required them to go through was designed to cure or rectify specific behavior. It was not designed to harm them, in point of fact God gave them specific instructions concerning what steps to take to ensure that they would not only survive but thrive during their process.

The next point I want to make is our desire does not control the duration of the process. No one wants to endure hardship and difficulties, in fact much of our time, energy and effort is spent attempting to ensure that we will face as little difficulty as possible. The only problem is that sometimes our desire to avoid difficulty can hinder our destiny. In fact it is often in the most difficult moments of our lives the times we most want to avoid, times of hardship and even despair that we both find God and learn to trust and depend on Him and without those moments our commitment to trust Him simply would not exist. If we were to examine the live of the most successful men and women though out history we would discover that many if not most of them suffered great personal difficulty prior to reaching the pinnacle of success. Even the stories of men and women in the Bible demonstrate that enduring difficulties is a prerequisite to true success. In the 3rd through 5th verses of the 5th Chapter of the Book of Romans, the Apostle Paul speaking on the value of difficulties in the life of a believer wrote " and not only so, but we glory in tribulations also: knowing that tribulations worketh patience: and patience, experience: and experience hope: and hope maketh not ashamed; because the love of God is shed abroad in our hearts by the Holy Ghost which is given unto us" In this scripture the Apostle Paul was providing insight into how a believer ought to view the difficulties that they endure. In reading these passage of scripture it should become evident that when we are experiencing difficulties in our lives our focus should be on the positive affect the experience will have upon our lives and not, or at least not solely, on the difficulty itself. Further, while admittedly this may be difficult it will better enable us to endure the difficulty we face without becoming fearful or bitter towards God or the people through whom the difficulty may come. I think It is helpful during times of difficulty to remember that good will always come from every circumstance or situation we find ourselves in and no event in our lives is pointless or senseless but rather they all have a purpose even if do not understand them at the time, or as the Apostle Paul wrote in the 28th and 29th verses of the 8th Chapter of the Book of Romans when he declared " and we know that all things work together for good to them that love God, to them who are the called according to his purpose. For whom he did foreknow, he also did predestinate to be conformed to the image of his son, that he might be the firstborn among many brethren." In other words everything that happens in our lives happens and is used to conform us into the image of Jesus. I think this subject why difficulties occur in the lives of believers is one of the least taught and most misunderstood subjects in the Bible. Many believe that any difficulty in our lives is a result of sin or a lack of faith and as a result see difficulty as an event to avoid and if not avoid to shorten the duration of the to greatest extent possible. It is quite natural to desire a pleasant life free of pain, sorrow and difficulty and I understand the appeal that the various teachings that suggest that the proper conduct and the proper confessions of faith will allow believers to avoid difficulties has on the body of Christ, however they are simply not true and more importantly they are not of God. In the 2nd verse of the 15th Chapter of the Gospel according to Saint John, Jesus declared "Every branch in me that bareth not fruit he taketh away: and every branch that bareth fruit, he pruneth it that it may bring forth more fruit" which at least implies that the difficulties that we face are not punishment but preparation for greater productivity in the Kingdom of God. In addition, one of, if not the most important understandings that we should get from this scripture is that it is God and not fate that controls our circumstances and that our difficulties are designed for a purpose and that purpose is to make us more like Jesus, which also means that our desire to be free of difficulties does not impact their occurrence or their duration.

The next point that I want to make is that our process is designed to produce a specific result. In the 10th through 14th verses of the 29th Chapter of the Book of Jeremiah the Prophet Jeremiah declares "For thus saith the Lord, that after seventy years be accomplished at Babylon I will visit you, and perform my good word toward you, in causing you to return to this place. For I know the thoughts that I think towards you, saith the Lord, thoughts of peace, and not of evil, to give you an expected end. Then shall ye call upon me, and ye shall go and pray unto me, and I will hearken unto you. And ye shall seek me, and find me, when you shall search for me with all your heart. And I will be found of you, saith the Lord: And I will turn away your captivity, and I will gather you from all the nations, and from all the places whither I have driven you, saith the Lord; and I will bring you again into the place whence I caused you to be carried away captive" In these passages of scripture God through the Prophet Jeremiah re-affirms His intentions to bless the Nation of Israel as well as established the criteria upon which their deliverance from captivity will take place, As we these consider this text there is one general observation that I believe needs to be made in order for us to truly understand what God is saying, the symbolism of time. When the Bible uses measurements of time more often than not the measurement of time uses has a much larger meaning. For example when the Bible speaks of Moses being in the wilderness for forty years, Jesus being in the wilderness forty days, it raining forty days and forty nights these numbers speak to an earthly process, when the Bible recounts the fifty days between Jesus being hung on a cross and his ascension in to heaven it speaks to the process of grace and here when the Bible speaks to the Nation of Israel being in captivity for seventy years it speaks to the process of completion. Therefore a more literal understanding of the 10th verse of the 29th Chapter of the Book of Jeremiah for our purposes would be that when the completion of your process has been accomplished at Babylon I will visit you, and perform my good word towards you, in causing you to return to this place. If this were not true the 13th and 14th verses would serve as a contradiction. However, the larger point I need to make is that the 10th through 14th verses teach us that God delivered the Nation of Israel into Babylonian captivity to accomplish a specific purpose, and bases their return from captivity upon the accomplishment of that purpose. Moreover, this is just as true with us as it was with the Nation of Israel. Each of us are called by God to a specific destiny and are given specific personality traits, gifts, abilities, and talents to enable us to fulfill our destiny, however in many instances we find ourselves focused more in the world around us that we are on the destiny that God established for us and live lives that look more like the world that they do like Jesus. Furthermore, tragically we find ourselves having greater affection for and trust in the things of this world than we do the things of God, In short our love for God has been replaced by a love for other things, and this is what our process is designed to correct. For some it is a desire for earthly success, for others still it is willfulness and rebellion, for others it is the pride of life, but whatever the obstacle is the process we go through is designed to remove it and return God to His rightful place in our lives. It should comes as comfort to know that the difficulties we face are not random, that they are not the result of some uncontrollable force plotting to destroy us, but rather are part of the plan of a loving father correcting the self destructive behavior of His children He loves so that they can become all that they were ordained to be and live in peace and harmony with Him and one another. This point is made clear in the 2nd through 5th verses of the 8th chapter of the Book of Deuteronomy the Bible which declares "and thou shalt remember all the ways which the Lord thy God led thee these forty years in the wilderness, to humble thee, and to prove thee, to know what was in thine heart, whether thou wouldest keep his commandments, or not. And he humbled thee, and suffered thee to hunger, and fed thee with manna, which thou knewest not, neither did thy fathers know; that he might make thee know that man doest not live by bread only, but by every word that proceedeth out of the mouth of the Lord doth man live. Thy raiment waxed not old upon thee, neither did thy foot swell, these forty years. Thou shalt also consider in thine heart, that as a man chasiteneth his son, so the Lord thy God chasiteneth thee." In other words I caused you to go through this process to test your heart and to teach you not to depend on the world but to depend upon me. As I read this scripture I hear an echo of the 1st and 2nd verses of the 12th Chapter of the Book of Romans which provides "I beseech you therefore, brethren, by the mercies of God, that ye present your bodies a living sacrifice, holy, acceptable unto God, which is your reasonable service. And be not conformed to this world: but be ye transformed by the renewing of your mind, that ye may prove what is the good, acceptable and perfect will of God." In this scripture the Apostle Paul sets forth the purpose of our process, that we be not conformed to this world but be transformed by the renewing of our minds. However what I think is equally important is the result of the process, prosperity. In the 2nd verse of the 12th Chapter of the Book of Romans the Apostle Paul teaches us that engaging in the process of being transformed will result in our demonstrating the good, and acceptable, and perfect will of God. This point is also echoed in the 6th through 18th verses of the 8th chapter of the Book of Deuteronomy which provides "Therefore thou shalt keep the commandments of the Lord thy God, to walk in his ways, and to fear him. For the Lord thy God bringeth thee into a good land, a land of brooks water, of fountains and depths that spring out of valleys and hills, a land of wheat, and barley, and vines, and figs trees, and pomegranates; a land of oil olive, and honey; and land wherein thou shalt eat bread without scarceness, thou shalt not lack any thing in it; a land whose stones are iron, and out of whose hills thou mayest dig brass, when thou hast eaten and art full, then thou shalt bless the Lord thy God for the good land which he hath given thee. Beware that thou forget not the Lord thy God, in not keeping his commandments, and his judgments, and his statutes, which I command thee this day: Let when thou has eaten and art full, and hast built goodly houses, and dwelt therein; and when thy heards and thy flocks multiplied, and all thy silver and thy gold is multiplied, and all that thou hast is multiplied then thine heart be lifted up, and thou forget the Lord thy God, which brought thee forth out of the land of Egypt, from the house of bondage; who led thee through that great and terrible wilderness, wherein were fiery serpents, and scorpions, and drought, where there was no water; who brought thee forth water out of the rock of flint; who fed thee in the wilderness with mamma, which thy fathers knew not, that he might humble thee, and that he might prove thee, to do thee good at the latter end; and thou say in thine heart, My power and the might of mine hand hath gotten me this wealth. But thou shalt remember the Lord thy God: for it is he that giveth thee power to get wealth, that he may establish his covenant which he sware unto the fathers, as it is this day." In both of these sets of scriptural passages God makes it clear that the process always produces prosperity but prosperity never proceeds the process. I think it is amazing that God is so loving and compassionate that not only does he provide a process that will allow us to proper but he also gives us assurances that one we complete our process that prosperity most certainly awaits. Jesus Himself spoke on this subject in the 24th through 33 rd verse of the 6th Chapter of Gospel according to Saint Matthew when He declared " No man can serve two masters: For either he will hate the one, and love the other; or else he will hold to the one, and despite the other. Ye cannot serve God and mammon. Therefore, I say unto you, take no through for your life, what ye shall eat, or what ye shall put on. Is not the life more than meat, and the body than raiment? Behold the fowls of the air: For they sow not, neither do they reap, nor gather into barns; yet your heavenly father feedeth them. Are ye not much better than they? Which of you by taking thought can add one cubit unto his statue? And why take ye thought for raiment? Consider the lilies of the Field, how they grow; they toil not, neither do thy spin: and yet I say unto you, that even Solomon in all his glory was not arrayed like one of these. Wherefore, if God so clothe the grass of the field, Which today is, and to morrow is cast into the oven, shall he not much more clothe you, O ye of little faith? Therefore, take no thought saying, what shall we eat? Or what shall we drink? Or wherewithal shall we be clothed?

(For after all these things do the Gentiles seek:) For your heavenly Father knoweth that Ye have need of all these things. But seek ye first the Kingdom of God and His righteousness; and all these things shall be added unto you." Can you see Jesus speaking about the uselessness of serving the world, can you hear the promise of prosperity that awaits the completion of the process. What more could we ask for than God himself promising us that he has designed for us all we need and all we have to do is comply and not protest. The final thing I want to mention is that it is our submission to the process and not the passage of time that determines if and when we will experience the prosperity promised. It amazes me how often we protest or rebel against God while He is attempting to take us through the process designed to prosper us without realizing the harm we are doing to ourselves and our destinies or how many of us risk forfeiting the very promise that defines our lives simply because we do not trust God enough to follow him. However, as tragic as this is it is not new and even the Nation of Israel suffered loss because their failure to trust God caused them to protest the very process God designed to prosper them. In the 2nd through 6th verses of the Book of Hebrews, speaking of the nations of Israel failure to obtain their promise wrote" For unto us was the gospel preached, as well as unto them: But the word preached did not profit them, not being mixed with faith in them that heard it. For we which have believed do enter into rest, as he said, as I have sworn in my wrath, if they shall enter into my rest: Although the works were finished from the foundation of the world. For he spake in a certain place of the seventh day on this wise, and God did rest the seventh day from all his works. And in this place again, if they shall enter into my rest. Seeing therefore it remaineth that some must enter therein, and they to whom it was first preached entered not in because of unbelief." In these passages of scripture the Apostle Paul is referring to the generation of the members of the Nation Israel who died in the wilderness because they did not trust God enough to bring them into their promise. In the 26th through 32 verses of the 13th Chapter of the Book of Numbers the Bible records the Nation of Israel's rebellion against God and provides "and they went and came to Moses, and to Aaron, and to all the congregation of the Children of Israel, unto the wilderness of Paran, to Kadesh; and brought back word unto them, and unto all the congregation, and shewed them the fruit of the land. And told him and said, we came unto the land whither thou sentest us, and surely it floweth with milk and honey; and this is the fruit of it. Nevertheless the people be strong that dwell in the land, and the cities are walled, and very great: and moreover we saw the children of Anak there. The Amalekites dwell in the land of the south: and the Hittites, and the Jubusites, and the Amorites, dwell in the mountains: and the Canaanites dwell by the sea, and by the coast of Jordan. And Caleb stilled the people before Moses, and said, Let us go up at once, and possess it; for we are well able to overcome it. But the men that went up with him said, we be not able to go up against the people; for they are stronger than we. And they brought up an evil report of the land which they had searched unto the Children of Israel, saying, the land through which we have gone to search it is a land that eateth up the inhabitants thereof; and all the people that we saw in it are men of a great stature." The thing that amazed me the most about this scripture is that all the signs and wonders that God performed in their presence and on their behalf were still not sufficient to produce faith or obedience in them, that despite God's faithfulness and generosity towards them they chose to rebel rather than comply, and what is worse is that there are in many in the Body of Christ today who respond to God the same way. On one hand they testify about God's goodness and on the other they rebel against His every command. The really tragic thing is that as much as it disturbs me, it disturbs God even more. In the 11th through 38th verses of the 14th Chapter of the Book of numbers the Bible records God's response and provides "And the LORD said unto Moses, How long will this people provoke me? and how long will it be ere they believe me, for all the signs which I have showed among them? I will smite them with the pestilence, and disinherit them, and will make of thee a greater nation and mightier than they. And Moses said unto the LORD, Then the Egyptians shall hear it, (for thou broughtest up this people in thy might from among them;) And they will tell it to the inhabitants of this land: for they have heard that thou LORD art among this people, that thou LORD art seen face to face, and that thy cloud standeth over them, and that thou goest before them, by day time in a pillar of a cloud, and in a pillar of fire by night. Now if thou shalt kill all this people as one man, then the nations which have heard the fame of thee will speak, saying, Because the LORD was not able to bring this people into the land which he sware unto them, therefore he hath slain them in the wilderness. And now, I beseech thee, let the power of my Lord be great, according as thou hast spoken, saying, The LORD is long-suffering, and of great mercy, forgiving iniquity and transgression, and by no means clearing the guilty, visiting the iniquity of the fathers upon the children unto the third and fourth generation. Pardon, I beseech thee, the iniquity of this people according unto the greatness of thy mercy, and as thou hast forgiven this people, from Egypt even until now.

And the LORD said, I have pardoned according to thy word: But as truly as I live, all the earth shall be filled with the glory of the LORD. Because all those men which have seen my glory, and my miracles, which I did in Egypt and in the wilderness, and have tempted me now these ten times, and have not hearkened to my voice; Surely they shall not see the land which I sware unto their fathers, neither shall any of them that provoked me see it: But my servant Caleb, because he had another spirit with him, and hath followed me fully, him will I bring into the land whereinto he went; and his seed shall possess it. (Now the Amalekites and the Canaanites dwelt in the valley.) Tomorrow turn you, and get you into the wilderness by the way of the Red sea. And the LORD spake unto Moses and unto Aaron, saying, How long shall I bear with this evil congregation, which murmur against me? I have heard the murmurings of the children of Israel, which they murmur against me. Say unto them, As truly as I live, saith the LORD, as ye have spoken in mine ears, so will I do to you: Your carcasses shall fall in this wilderness; and all that were numbered of you, according to your whole number, from twenty years old and upward which have murmured against me. Doubtless ye shall not come into the land, concerning which I sware to make you dwell therein, save Caleb the son of Jephunneh, and Joshua the son of Nun. But your little ones, which ye said should be a prey, them will I bring in, and they shall know the land which ye have despised. But as for you, your carcasses, they shall fall in this wilderness. And your children shall wander in the wilderness forty years, and bear your whoredoms, until your carcasses be wasted in the wilderness. After the number of the days in which ye searched the land, even forty days, each day for a year, shall ye bear your iniquities, even forty years, and ye shall know my breach of promise. I the LORD have said, I will surely do it unto all this evil congregation, that are gathered together against me: in this wilderness they shall be consumed, and there they shall die. And the men, which Moses sent to search the land, who returned, and made all the congregation to murmur against him, by bringing up a slander upon the land, Even those men that did bring up the evil report upon the land, died by the plague before the LORD. But Joshua the son of Nun, and Caleb the son of Jephunneh, which were of the men that went to search the land, lived still." It should be clear from reading these passages of scripture that no good ever comes from protesting God's process which is the essence of rebellion towards God. It should be equally clear that our protest against God's process for our lives does nothing but serve to delay the prosperity we desire because our prosperity is only released after our process is complete.

7.

ELEMENT SEVEN

The Believers understanding that they must learn to move in God's timing

God's timing is perfect in fact one of the greatest blessings of our faith is the ability to trust the timing of God. The Bible teaches us valuable lessons concerning the perfection of God's timing. God's timing is always perfect because God's knowledge is complete and God's intentions are pure, just and good, and as a result God desires the absolute best for us and knows exactly what that is in every situation and exactly when it should happen. We see a powerful discussion of God's timing in the 1st Chapter of the Book of Genesis. In the 1st through 28th verses of the 1st chapter of the Book of Genesis the Bible declares "In the beginning God created the heaven and the earth. And the earth was without form, and void; and darkness was upon the face of the deep. And the Spirit of God moved upon the face of the waters. And God said, Let there be light: and there was light. And God saw the light, that it was good: and God divided the light from the darkness. And God called the light day, and the darkness he called night. And the evening and the morning were the first day. And God said, Let there be a firmament in the midst of the waters, and let it divide the waters from the waters. And God made the firmament, and divided the waters which were under the firmament from the waters which were above the firmament: and it was so. And God called the firmament Heaven. And the evening and the morning were the second day. And God said, Let the waters under the heaven be gathered together unto one place, and let the dry land appear: and it was so. And God called the dry land Earth; and the gathering together of the waters called the Seas: and God saw that it was good. And God said, Let the earth bring forth grass, the herb yielding seed, and the fruit tree yielding fruit after his kind, whose seed is in itself, upon the earth: and it was so. And the earth brought forth grass, and herb yielding seed after his kind, and the tree yielding fruit, whose seed was in itself, after his kind: and God saw that it was good. And the evening and the morning were the third day. And God said, Let there be lights in the firmament of the heaven to divide the day from the night; and let them be for signs, and for seasons, and for days, and years: and let them be for lights in the firmament of the heaven to give light upon the earth: and it was so. And God made two great lights; the greater light to rule the day, and the lesser light to rule the night: he made the stars also. And God set them in the firmament of the heaven to give light upon the earth, and to rule over the day and over the night, and to divide the light from the darkness: and God saw that it was good. And the evening and the morning were the fourth day. And God said, Let the waters bring forth abundantly the moving creature that hath life, and fowl that may fly above the earth in the open firmament of heaven. And God created great whales, and every living creature that moveth, which the waters brought forth abundantly, after their kind, and every winged fowl after his kind: and God saw that it was good. And God blessed them, saying, Be fruitful, and multiply, and fill the waters in the seas, and let fowl multiply in the earth. And the evening and the morning were the fifth day. And God said, Let the earth bring forth the living creature after his kind, cattle, and creeping thing, and beast of the earth after his kind: and it was so. And God made the beast of the earth after his kind, and cattle after their kind, and every thing that creepeth upon the earth after his kind: and God saw that it was good. And God said, Let us make man in our image, after our likeness: and let them have dominion over the fish of the sea, and over the fowl of the air, and over the cattle, and over all the earth, and over every creeping thing that creepeth upon the earth. So God created man in His own image, in the image of God created He him; male and female created He them. And God blessed them, and God said unto them, Be fruitful, and multiply, and replenish the earth, and subdue it: and have dominion over the fish of the sea, and over the fowl of the air, and over every living thing that moveth upon the earth" In examining these passages of scripture it becomes evident that God's timing is an expression of God's order and that each act of God's sovereign will serves as a stepping stone for the next. I think the order in which God does things is astonishing. How God created light which produces heat, which in turn caused the firmaments to divide, and uncover the dry ground, then brought forth the grass, the herb yielding seed, and the trees yielding fruit. How God then created the sun, stars and moon to divide the day from the night and in so doing created an ecologically balanced environment that would sustain itself even to the point that plants produce oxygen in the day and consume it at night. How God then caused the waters to bring forth life after He created air for them to breathe and food for them to (plant life) eat. It is amazing how God created everything in the exact time and placed it in the exact order and then created a man to rule over it and keep it. Much less how everything that Adam needed to fulfill his destiny was established in the exact timing and exact order required for the perfect result to occur. This fact should provide great comfort to those who truly desire God's will for their lives and strengthen their commitment to trust and follow God.

Sadly, there are still those in the Body of Christ that have not yet developed the trust and faith in God and His word needed to rest in the knowledge that God's timing is perfect and instead seem to ignore the evidence and refuse to trust God and rest in Him. In the 1st through 7th verses of the 4th Chapter of the Book of Hebrews, the Apostle Paul spoke of the danger of not resting in God's timing when he declared "Let us therefore fear, lest, a promise being left us of entering into his rest, any of you should seem to come short of it. For unto us was the gospel preached, as well as unto them: but the word preached did not profit them, not being mixed with faith in them that heard it. For we which have believed do enter into rest, as He said, As I have sworn in my wrath, if they shall enter into my rest: although the works were finished from the foundation of the world. For He spake in a certain place of the seventh day on this wise, And God did rest the seventh day from all his works. And in this place again, If they shall enter into my rest. Seeing therefore it remaineth that some must enter therein, and they to whom it was first preached entered not in because of unbelief: again, He limiteth a certain day, saying in David, Today, after so long a time; as it is said, Today if ye will hear His voice, harden not your hearts" In these scriptures the Apostle Paul expressed great concern that we receive God's promises of rest from our labors and enter into His rest and avoid the failure of those who did not entered into God's rest because of their lack of faith. What becomes obvious to me as I consider this scripture is how important entering into God's rest is as well as how grave our failure to enter in is for our lives and the lives of so many countless others. It should be clear to each of us that God established a plan for our lives and in God's plan there is both an assignment and a blessing which are linked together and released according to God's timing. It should also be clear that waiting on God's timing is what the Apostle Paul refers to as entering into God's rest. When we trust God to truly be the head of our lives we recognize that not only does God have a plan for our lives but God's plan is what is best for us and that God will perform it in His order and His timing. Our failure to trust either that God's plan is best for us or that God will perform it in His order and according to His timing produces both resentment and rebellion in us and is a mark of our lack of spiritual maturity. It also produces frustration and worry. In the 24th through 34th verses of the 6th Chapter of the Gospel according to Saint Matthew Jesus speaks directly to the subject of resting in God's timing when He declared "No man can serve two masters: for either he will hate the one, and love the other; or else he will hold to the one, and despise the other. Ye cannot serve God and mammon. Therefore I say unto you, Take no thought for your life, what ye shall eat, or what ye shall drink; nor yet for your body, what ye shall put on. Is not the life more than meat, and the body than raiment? Behold the fowls of the air: for they sow not, neither do they reap, nor gather into barns; yet your heavenly Father feedeth them. Are ye not much better than they? Which of you by taking thought can add one cubit unto his stature? And why take ye thought for raiment? Consider the lilies of the field, how they grow; they toil not, neither do they spin: and yet I say unto you, That even Solomon in all his glory was not arrayed like one of these. Wherefore, if God so clothe the grass of the field, which today is, and tomorrow is cast into the oven, shall He not much more clothe you, O ye of little faith? Therefore take no thought, saying, What shall we eat? or, What shall we drink? or, Wherewithal shall we be clothed? (For after all these things do the Gentiles seek:) for your heavenly Father knoweth that ye have need of all these things. But seek ye first the kingdom of God, and His righteousness; and all these things shall be added unto you. Take therefore no thought for the morrow: for the morrow shall take thought for the things of itself. Sufficient unto the day is the evil thereof" In these passages of scripture there a number of things which I believe need to be addressed. The first is Jesus statement found in the 24th verse "No man can serve two Masters". One of the major themes in the Bible is that there are two forces battling for control of the heart and soul of mankind, one of which is carnal and fleshly and one that is spiritual and Godly and that each of us must chose. Each of us must decide whether we will devote, the life, time, energy, resources and gifts given to us by God to build the Kingdoms of this world or the kingdom of God. While for many in the Body of Christ this distinction has been blurred it is crystal clear in the sight of God. In point of fact Jesus speaks to the clarity with which God views the need to choose in the 30 the verse of the 12th Chapter of the Gospel according to Saint Matthew when He declared "he that is not with me is against me; and he that gathereth not with me scattereth abroad." In other words all those who serve mammon are opposed or against Jesus and all those that serve Him are with Jesus. This point is further highlighted in the 15th and 16th verses of the 2nd chapter of the 1st epistle of John where it provides Love not the world, neither the things of the world. If any man loves the world, the love of the Father is not in him. For all that is in the world, the lust of the flesh, and the lust of the eye, and the pride of life, is not of the Father, but is of the world" In both these passages of scripture the Bible warns of the danger of becoming focused on obtaining the things of this world and placing the acquisition and accumulation of them above the will of God and God's purpose for our lives. However, I think the greatest admonishment comes from Jesus' statement found in the 32nd verse of the 6th Gospel according to Saint Matthew when Jesus speaking of the focus on material things declared " for after these things do the gentles seek" Just imagine how God sees those Christians who are consumed with obtaining the things of this world and have as their goal the obtaining worldly success, whether in the form of fame, a career, the accumulation of wealth, power, personal fulfillment to the point where it has become more important to them than the fulfilling their God given destinies. In point of fact Jesus addressed this issue in the 34th through 37th verses of the 8th Chapter of the Gospel according to Saint Mark where it provides "And when he had called the people unto him with his disciples also, he said unto them, Whosoever will come after me, let him deny himself, and take up his cross, and follow me. For whosoever will save his life shall lose it; but whosoever shall lose his life for my sake and the gospel's, the same shall save it. For what shall it profit a man, if he shall gain the whole world, and lose his own soul? Or what shall a man give in exchange for his soul? "In this passage of scripture Jesus raises the question of priority and value and asks us to examine what has greater value, the life we may desire to create based on our will and power or the life He calls us to lead based on His will and His power. For those who do not know God, have not received the amazing gift of salvation, who cannot see the hand of God moving in their lives or the will of God taking shape before them or have not been touched be the life altering expression of God's love, (the gentiles) I understand that the pursuit of the things of this would being their priority and what they value because it is all then know and all they can serve is mammon, but what about us, those who have experienced the gift of salvation, the unending expressions of God love, how could we who have been given so much still choice our will over His, how could we act like those who do not believe what we profess so loudly? Perhaps it is because we have not matured, have not taken the advise of the Apostle Paul found in the 1st and 2nd verses of the 12th Chapter of the Book of Romans where he writes "I beseech you therefore, brethren, by the mercies of God, that ye present your bodies a living sacrifice, holy, acceptable unto God, which is your reasonable service. And be not conformed to this world: but be ye transformed by the renewing of your mind, that ye may prove what is that good, and acceptable, and perfect will of God" or as the amplified translation states "I appeal to you therefore, brethren, *and* beg of you in view of [all] the mercies of God, to make a decisive dedication of your bodies [presenting all your members and faculties] as a living sacrifice, holy (devoted, consecrated) and well pleasing to God, which is your reasonable (rational, intelligent) service *and* spiritual worship. ² Do not be conformed to this world (this age), [fashioned after and adapted to its external, superficial customs], but be transformed (changed) by the [entire] renewal of your mind [by its new ideals and its new attitude], so that you may prove [for yourselves] what is the good and acceptable and perfect will of God, *even* the thing which is good and acceptable and perfect [in His sight for you]." It is the act of presenting your body as a living sacrifice that begins the process of Christian Maturity and this process of renewing our minds the changing of our ideas and attitudes that separates us from the gentiles and allows us to gather with Christ and not scatter abroad, to no longer be lovers of the world and to begin to serve God and not mammon. But this act of making a decisive dedication of our entire bodies requires faith not only in the existence of God but in His willingness to provide. This brings me to my next point, God will provide for us.

In the 6th through 31st verses of the 6th Chapter of the Gospel according to Saint Matthew provides "But thou, when thou prayest, enter into thy closet, and when thou hast shut thy door, pray to thy Father which is in secret; and thy Father which seeth in secret shall reward thee openly. But when ye pray, use not vain repetitions, as the heathen do: for they think that they shall be heard for their much speaking. Be not ye therefore like unto them: for your Father knoweth what things ye have need of, before ye ask him. After this manner therefore pray ye: Our Father which art in heaven, Hallowed be thy name. Thy kingdom come. Thy will be done in earth, as it is in heaven. Give us this day our daily bread. And forgive us our debts, as we forgive our debtors. And lead us not into temptation, but deliver us from evil: for thine is the kingdom, and the power, and the glory, Amen. For if ye forgive men their trespasses, your heavenly Father will also forgive you: but if ye forgive not men their trespasses, neither will your Father forgive your trespasses. Moreover, when ye fast, be not, as the hypocrites, of a sad countenance: for they disfigure their faces, that they may appear unto men to fast. Verily I say unto you, They have their reward. But thou, when thou fastest, anoint thine head, and wash thy face; that thou appear not unto men to fast, but unto thy Father which is in secret: and thy Father which seeth in secret shall reward thee openly. Lay not up for yourselves treasures upon earth, where moth and rust doth corrupt, and where thieves break through and steal: but lay up for yourselves treasures in heaven, where neither moth nor rust doth corrupt, and where thieves do not break through nor steal: for where your treasure is, there will your heart be also. The light of the body is the eye: if therefore thine eye be single, thy whole body shall be full of light. But if thine eye be evil, thy whole body shall be full of darkness. If therefore the light that is in thee be darkness, how great is that darkness! No man can serve two masters: for either he will hate the one, and love the other; or else he will hold to the one, and despise the other. Ye cannot serve God and mammon. Therefore I say unto you, Take no thought for your life, what ye shall eat, or what ye shall drink; nor yet for your body, what ye shall put on. Is not the life more than meat, and the body than raiment? Behold the fowls of the air: for they sow not, neither do they reap, nor gather into barns; yet your heavenly Father feedeth them. Are ye not much better than they? Which of you by taking thought can add one cubit unto his stature? And why take ye thought for raiment?

Consider the lilies of the field, how they grow; they toil not, neither do they spin: and yet I say unto you, That even Solomon in all his glory was not arrayed like one of these. Wherefore, if God so clothe the grass of the field, which today is, and tomorrow is cast into the oven, shall he not much more clothe you, O ye of little faith? Therefore take no thought, saying, What shall we eat? or, What shall we drink? or, Wherewithal shall we be clothed? Jesus teaches us the importance of placing a greater priority on our spiritual life than the pursuit of world matters and while so doing ask a series of questions which serve two purposes. The first is to demonstrate the care God takes in providing for His creation (especially Man) and the second is to make clear how pointless our efforts are to provide for or to protect ourselves are in our own power. It is the first of these two points that I want to focus on. Through out scripture God promises to not only provide for those who trust and obey Him but the Bible is filled with examples of God's intervention in the lives of men to provide for and bless them. In point of fact it is God's record of intervention in the lives of His people that the Apostle Paul describes as the mercies of God. If we are honest with ourselves, we have ample evidence of God's intervention in our lives, whether it is the healing of our bodies, the mending of relationships, God's act of bring or removing the right people at the moment, or God moving in circumstances that seemed impossible for us, that should develop within us not only an unshakable faith, but an unmovable resolve to follow God. However, for those of whom that is still not enough God issues an invitation to stand in His promises, which is the essence of our faith. Whether it is the promise of provision contained in the 19th verse of the 1st Chapter of the Book of Isaiah which declares "if you are willing and obedient, ye shall eat the good of the land" or the promise of overwhelming blessings contained in the 1st and 2nd verses of the 28th Chapter of the Book of Deuteronomy which provides " and it shall come to pass, if thou shalt hearken diligently unto the voice of the Lord thy God, to observe and to do all his commandments which I have commanded thee this day, that the Lord thy God will set thee on high above all nations of the earth: and all theses blessings shall come on thee, and overtake thee, if thou shalt hearken unto the voice of the Lord thy God" or the promises of reward found in the 6th verse of the 11th Chapter of the Book of Hebrews which provides " But without God it is impossible to please Him: for He that cometh to God must believe that He is, and that he is a rewarder of them that diligently seek him." or even the promise contained in the 33rd verse of the 6th Chapter of the Gospel according to Saint Matthew which provides " But seek ye first the

Kingdom of God and His righteousness and all these things will be added unto you" we must recognize that God's promises are subject to God's timing. These scriptures are only a small portion of the promises of God's provision and blessings contained in the Bible all of which were written to provide us with the assurance that God is both able and willing to provide for those that trust and rest in Him. However, if we were to examine each of these as well as countless of God's other promises it would become evident that these promises will be fulfilled in God's timing and in furtherance of God's order. Which brings me to the final point that becomes clear from Jesus' teaching in the 6th through 34th verses of the 6th Chapter of the Gospel according to Saint Matthew, that God's timing is connected to God's order. If we were to examine the 33rd verse of the 6th Chapter of the Gospel according to Saint Matthew, the 6th verse of the 11th Chapter of the Book of

Hebrews, the 19th verse of the 1st Chapter of the Book of Isaiah or any other of the various passages of scripture which contain God's promises of protection, provision or blessings it would become evident that God's protection, provision and blessings follow a pattern and are always preceded by certain preconditions which must be met by the person receiving them. One of the clearest examples of this point is found in the story of Abram contained in the Book of Genesis. In the 1st through 4th verses of the 12th Chapter of the Book of Genesis the Bible provides "Now the LORD had said unto Abram, Get thee out of thy country, and from thy kindred, and from thy father's house, unto a land that I will show thee: and I will make of thee a great nation, and I will bless thee, and make thy name great; and thou shalt be a blessing: and I will bless them that bless thee, and curse him that curseth thee: and in thee shall all families of the earth be blessed. So Abram departed, as the LORD had spoken unto him; and Lot went with him: and Abram was seventy and five years old when he departed out of Haran." In this scripture we see God promise Abram not only a child but a great nation would be birthed through him. I cannot imagine the sense of excitement that Abram must have felt hearing that God was going to provide him with a seed and that what he (Abram), could not produce with his own power God would produce for him. However, I am sure that Abram never thought that he would be close to 100 years old at the time God produced the child of his promise or over four hundred years before the promise of a great nation would be fulfilled. Further, if Abram had his way the promises of God would have been fulfilled immediately, however learning that God moves in His timing and not man's was a test of Abram's spiritual maturity, just as it is ours. In addition, just as it is with us Abram's period of waiting was not random but was connected to God's order. Each season Abram waited was marked by Abram's life moving further and further into God's order, first the step of specific obedience, where Abram saw the consequence of bring Lot with him instead of leaving Lot behind as his obedience would have required. The next step of trust was where Abram has to learn that God was his protector and provider, as Abram fled the famine and surrendered Sarah only to be rescued by God, then there was the test of faith when Abram failing to believe that God could do what man could not, conceived a child with Hagar believing that God required his help in fulfilling God's promise. All of which culminated in Abram's determination that only God would be his source as he refused to receive a blessing from the King of Sodom and determined that His blessings would only come form God. Abram's process of maturity was further demonstrated as he passed the of submission when he chose to honor God with his tithe by placing them in the hands of the priest Melchezedek, then and only then did the promises of God began to come to pass. How are you doing with the steps God designed for you? Through each of these events Abram was taught by God to trust God's order and timing, which is the principle requirement needed to enter into God's rest. If we as members of the Body of Christ would recognize the faithfulness of God our learning to move in His timing instead of our own would be simple and we would truly see the beauty of God's plan for our lives. We would also spare ourselves a great deal of heart ache and loss which results from taking matters into our own hands and moving out of God's will. Just think about all the mistakes that could have been avoided if we could only learn to wait on God. In the 6th and 7th verses of the 4th Chapter of the Book of Philippians the Apostle Paul instructs the Church "be careful for nothing; but in everything by prayer and supplication with thanksgiving let your requests be made known to God, and the peace of God, which passeth all understanding, shall keep your hearts and minds through Christ Jesus" In these of scriptures I believe that the Apostle Paul has given us the key to learning to move in God's timing prayer and thanksgiving. I realize that it may seem to some that prayer and thanksgiving have little to do with moving in God's timing however I believe that if we take a look at how these passages of scripture read in the amplified translation my point becomes clear, the amplified translation reads "do not fret or have any anxiety about anything, but in every circumstance and in everything by prayer and petition [definite requests] with thanksgiving continue to make your wants known to God. And God's peace [be yours, that tranquil state of the soul assured of its salvation through Christ and so fearing nothing from God and content with its earthly lot of whatever sort that is, that peace] which transcends all understanding, shall garrison and mount guard over your hearts and minds in Christ Jesus". What these passages of scripture are telling us is that if we focus our attention on God as our source of whatever we need or desire God will give us peace (a calm assurance) concerning the outcome and as long as we hold onto the peace of God it will remove the worry (fear concerning the outcome) that so often compels us to act on our own instead of moving in God's timing. As we consider the importance of remaining in prayer concerning those things that concern us I would like to remind you of the question that Jesus asked in the 27th verse of the 6th Chapter of the Gospel according to Saint Matthew" which of you by taking thought can add one cubit unto his stature" or as the amplified translation states " and which of you by worrying and being anxious can add one unit of measure [cubit] to his stature or to the span of his life?" what Jesus is asking simply out is and what each of us who struggle with waiting for God's timing must ask ourselves, is what can we really accomplish without God? Whenever I feel myself developing the urge to take matters into my own hands or the urge to create a solution with my own mind, I ask my self what is it that I think I can accomplish with out God and I realize the need to pray for God's peace in that situation as I sit still and wait on God's timing. Whenever I think about the power of moving in God's timing I cannot help but think about the story of the Nation of Israel's crossing into the promise land. In the 1st through 17th verses of the 3rd Chapter of the Book of Joshua the Bible provides "And Joshua rose early in the morning; and they removed from Shittim, and came to Jordan, he and all the children of Israel, and lodged there before they passed over. And it came to pass after three days, that the officers went through the host; and they commanded the people, saying, When ye see the ark of the covenant of the LORD your God, and the priests the Levites bearing it, then ye shall remove from your place, and go after it. Yet there shall be a space between you and it, about two thousand cubits by measure: come not nearer unto it that ye may know the way by which ye must go: for ye have not passed this way heretofore. And Joshua said unto the people, sanctify yourselves: for tomorrow the LORD will do wonders among you. And Joshua spake unto the priests, saying, Take up the Ark of the Covenant, and pass over before the people. And they took up the Ark of the Covenant, and went before the people. And the LORD said unto Joshua, This day will I begin to magnify thee in the sight of all Israel, that they may know that, as I was with Moses, so I will be with thee. And thou shalt command the priests that bear the Ark of the Covenant, saying, when ye are come to the brink of the water of Jordan, ye shall stand still in Jordan. And Joshua said unto the children of Israel, Come hither, and hear the words of the LORD your God. And Joshua said, Hereby ye shall know that the living God is among you, and that he will without fail drive out from before you the Canaanites, and the Hittites, and the Hivites, and the Per'izzites, and the Gir'gashites, and the Amorites, and the Jeb'usites. Behold, the ark of the covenant of the Lord of all the earth passeth over before you into Jordan. Now therefore take you twelve men out of the tribes of Israel, out of every tribe a man. And it shall come to pass, as soon as the soles of the feet of the priests that bear the ark of the LORD, the Lord of all the earth, shall rest in the waters of Jordan, that the waters of Jordan shall be cut off from the waters that come down from above; and they shall stand upon a heap. And it came to pass, when the people removed from their tents, to pass over Jordan, and the priests bearing the ark of the covenant before the people; and as they that bare the ark were come unto Jordan, and the feet of the priests that bare the ark were dipped in the brim of the water, (for Jordan over floweth all his banks all the time of harvest,) that the waters which came down from above stood and rose up upon a heap very far from the city Adam, that is beside Zar'etan; and those that came down toward the sea of the plain, even the salt sea, failed, and were cut off: and the people passed over right against Jericho. And the priests that bare the ark of the covenant of the LORD stood firm on dry ground in the midst of Jordan, and all the Israelites passed over on dry ground, until all the people were passed clean over Jordan." As I read this story there are a few things that I believe merit discussion, the first is that moving in God's timing requires preparation. In the 5th verse of the 3rd Chapter of the Book of Joshua, Joshua instructed the People "sanctify yourselves: for to morrow the Lord will do wonders among you" sanctification is a process through which the person being sanctified separates themselves of everything that is unclean or defiled in the sight of God. Furthermore, while it is often represented in the old testament as an act of physical cleaning it is more literally, repenting, renouncing or divorcing oneself from those ideas, values, desires and customers that are contrary to God's word. In the 17th and 18th verses of the 15th Chapter of the 2nd Book of Corinthians the Apostle Paul wrote "Therefore, if any man be in Christ, he is a new creature: old things are passed away; behold, all things are becomes new. And all things are of God, who hath reconciled us to himself by Jesus Christ, And hath given to us the ministry of reconciliation" and in so doing paints a clear picture of what it means to sanctify oneself. In addition, the Apostle Paul also spoke on the subject of sanctification in the 1st and 2nd verses of the 12th Chapter of the Book of Romans when he wrote " I beseech you therefore, brethren, by the mercies of God, that ye present your bodies a living sacrifice, Holy, acceptable unto God, which is you reasonable service. And be not conformed to this world: but be ye transformed by the renewing of your mind, that ye might prove what is that good, and acceptable, and perfect will of God." In other words sanctification is the process of allowing your mind to be renewed by the word of God. This is vital because it is only as we begin to transform our minds do we have any hope of moving in God's timing.

The next point I want to make is that God's timing establishes God's order. In the 2nd through 4th verses of the 3rd Chapter of the Book of Joshua, Joshua declared "and it came to pass after three days, that the officers went through the hosts; and they commanded the people, saying, when ye see the Ark of the Covenant of the Lord your God. And the priests the Levites bearing it, then ye shall remove from your place. And go after it. Yet there shall be a space between you and it, about two thousand cubits by measure: come not nearer unto it, that ye may knowest the way by which ye must go: for ye have not passed this way heretofore." Here we see God through His servant Joshua establish the order in which they were to move, notice that not only did God establish the order in which they were to move, but the distance between them. If we are going to learn to move in God's timing we must understand the need to take our cues from God. I have all ways found it interesting that God makes no mention of the personal desires of the people, how tired of waiting they must have been, the magnitude of their need or any of the things that we believe should effect God's timing but instead said "when ye see the ark of the covenant of the Lord your God, and the priests the Levites bearing it, then ye shall remove from your place. And go after it", In other words, when you see God move then it is time for you to move, I think it bares mentioning that the ark of the covenant contained a jar of the Manna which God provided for them in the wilderness, a portion of Aaron's budded staff, which represented God's power and the tablets which contained the ten commandments handed down to Moses by God, because God's timing is an expression of God's power or God's provision in an manner which is consistent with God's laws, and at no point should we as members of the Body of Christ allow ourselves to believe that something is in God's timing if there is not provision, no evidence of God's power or it will result in a violation of God's laws.

The next point I want to discuss is that God's timing will produces something new. In the 4th verse of the 3rd Chapter of the Book of Joshua the Bible reads "Yet there shall be a space between you and it, about two thousand cubits by measure: come not nearer unto it, that ye may knoweth the way by which ye must go: for ye have not passed this way heretofore." In other words you have not seen where I am taking you or how you are going to get there. This should come as great news for all of those who are waiting on God to move in any area of your life. In the 8th and 9th verses of the 55th Chapter of the Book of Isaiah God through the Prophet Isaiah declared "for my thoughts are not your thoughts, neither are your ways my ways saith the Lord. For as the heavens are higher than the earth, so are my ways higher than your ways, and my thoughts than your thoughts." In these verses of scripture God makes it clear that God does not think or view things like we do.

The things we see as difficult are not difficult for God, God recognizes no lack. No limitations and no hindrances the way we do. God's ways are always the best and most effective way to accomplish what is best to accomplish. When I think about the circumstances that the Nation of Israel found themselves facing in the 3rd Chapter of the Book of Joshua I ask myself what I would have done, there a number of very good ideas that come to mind, since they were in the wilderness, they could have built a fleet of boats and sail across the Jordan, they could have found a shallow point in the rives and swam or waded across, they could have waited until the dry season when the river was lower and calmer. However, none of these ideas were as good or as effective as God's idea of parting the Jordan. It is possible that depending on your particular background and experience you may have considered solutions better than mine, maybe you thought of building a bridge so they could use it to walk over the Jordan, or maybe even build a damn up stream and try to halt the flow of the Jordan long enough for the Nation of Israel to cross over. However, your thoughts or ideas while perhaps better than mine would still not have been as good or as effective as God's and perhaps more importantly yours like mine include a margin of error and the possibility of failure but God's do not because God's ways are perfect. Just think for a moment what could be a more perfect solution that to simply cause the water to part and the river bed to be dry, but of course only God could bring that solution to pass because only God has the power to hold back the water.

This brings me to my next point, God's timing releases God's power. In the 5th verse of the 3rd Chapter of the Book of Joshua the Bible declares "And Joshua said unto the people, sanctify yourselves: for to morrow the Lord will do wonders among you" I believe the greatest test that we as members of the Body of Christ face is whether we will wait on God or will we take matters into our own hands. Because if we take matters into our own hands we will never see God's power moves in our lives. I think this is the greatest tragedy of the modern Church that we are so unwillingly to wait on God that we do not experience His power and what the world is waiting for are those who are witnesses of His power. Can you picture how different Daniel's story would be if he had taken matters into his own hands and refrained from praying for thirty days in accordance with decree of king Darius, what would his testimony be, that because he did not trust God's power to deliver him from the hands of a man or a creature God created so he honored a man above God in order to save himself. I shutter to think how many of our lives actually tell that story, I did not trust God so I did it myself or what if Meshach, Shadrach and Abednego decided that God was not able to deliver them from the fiery furnace so they chose to worship Nebuchadnezzar instead of God: what would the testimony of their lives be if they did not exercise the maturity to wait on God's timing. In each of these instances and countless others ordinary men and women just like you and I choose to wait for God's timing and not act in their own and in each case the result was the same God's timing released God's power and produced a solution that they had never seen before. Whatever, you are in need of, whatever you are facing I want to urge you to wait on God's timing because His ways are not our ways and His thoughts are not our thoughts and God can provide solutions that no one else can. One of the best examples I can think of to illustrate this point is the woman with the issue of blood. In the 25th through 34th verses of the 5th Chapter of the Gospel according to Saint Mark the

Bible recounts the story of the woman with the issue of blood and provides "And a certain woman, which had an issue of blood twelve years, And had suffered many things of many physicians, and had spent all that she had, and was nothing bettered, but rather grew worse, when she had heard of Jesus, came in the press behind, and touched his garment. For she said, If I may touch but his clothes, I shall be whole. And straightway the fountain of her blood was dried up; and she felt in her body that she was healed of that plague. And Jesus, immediately knowing in himself that virtue had gone out of him, turned him about in the press, and said, Who touched my clothes? And his disciples said unto him, Thou seest the multitude thronging thee, and sayest thou, Who touched me? And he looked round about to see her that had done this thing. But the woman fearing and trembling, knowing what was done in her, came and fell down before Him, And told Him all the truth. And He said unto her, Daughter, thy faith hath made thee whole; go in peace, and be whole of thy plague." In this scripture I see a picture of the lives of so many in the Body of Christ, those who having placed their faith in the systems and knowledge of the world to solve the most important and even life threatening problems only to waste valuable time, energy and resources while the problem continues to get worse. Many would say that they like the woman with the issue of blood, had no choice because relying on God was not possible under the circumstances and the urgency of the situation and the potential for dire consequences made it necessary to rely on the things that were available at the time. However the reality of their lives is much the same as the woman with the issue of blood, what we determine to be necessary not only failed to solve the problem but in actuality made matters worse. For some this truth may be hard to see and even harder to accept but the truth remains the same. That the steps we take and the decisions we made to protect, provide for and bless ourselves are in truth destroying us. The ability to understand and accept this truth will only come with spiritual maturity. In the 35th and 36th verses of the 8th Chapter of the Gospel according to Saint Mark Jesus in teaching His disciples says something that we all need to consider " For whosoever will save his life will lose it: but whosoever shall lose his life for my sake and the gospel's sake the same shall save it. For what shall it profit a man if he shall gain the whole world, and lose his own soul?" These passages of scripture raise an important question if you obtain what you desire but have to move without God to get it, is it worth it in the first place? As I close this chapter there is something that I pray that you will consider, many in the modern Church have begun to focus their attention and even their ministries on the articulations in scripture such as the 10th verse of the 10th Chapter of the Gospel according to Saint John where Jesus declared "The thief cometh not, but for to steal, and to kill, and to destroy: I am come that they might have life, and that they might have it more abundantly" as a means of emphasizing God's desire that we all have a blessed and enjoyable life. However, what many have forgotten is there is no greater blessing nor is there any greater source of Joy that being in the will of God. So if you are seeking something that will require you to move in your timing and not God's to obtain it, can it possibly be a blessing.

8.

ELEMENT EIGHT

The believers understanding that their praise and worship of God is to be based on who God is and not what God does.

In the 4th and 5th verses of the 100th division of Psalms the psalmist wrote "enter into his gates with thanksgiving, and into his courts with praise: be thankful unto him, and bless his name. For the Lord is good; and his mercy is everlasting; and his truth endureth to all generations." In this scripture the psalmist instructs us to do two things the first is to enter into his gates with thanksgiving and the second is to enter into his courts with praise. On first blush, these two instructions might appear to be redundant because in the modern Church, the discussion of thanksgiving has faded away and has been replaced with a sense of expectation and entitlement, and praise has been transformed into an expression of approval. In our culture, (that is the Culture of the Church), God's identity has be so closely linked with His performance that the truth of His nature has all but been lost, and as a result we have lost our sense of perspective concerning who God is, we have become so comfortable with the concept of God as father, (daddy) that we have loss touch with His sovereignty, His holiness, His goodness, His generosity. We have lost sight of God Himself in the midst of His activity. In the 4th and 5th verses of the 100th psalm the author speaks to us about the way we must approach God and the order in which we must see God and perhaps more importantly the way we mature in God. As we first come to acknowledge the existence of God, God reveals His nature through His activity in fact God created all that exists in the created world so that we would come to know Him. God recognizing our inability to recognize Him in His absolute and pure essence chose to express His nature through activities to which we could relate. God gives us provision in abundance so that we will recognize that He is a provider and that He is generous, God shields us and protects us so that will recognize that God is a protector, God forgives us so that we will recognize that He is merciful, comforts us so we will recognize that He is compassionate. Each of the specific acts of God both provide us with a specific gift and a general revelation for which God requires and deserves a response from us for each. For each gift we receive from Him we are to offer thanksgiving and for each attribute we have come to recognize about Him we are to give Him praise. Some might ask is there a difference or perhaps more appropriately what is the difference. Imagine for a moment you are visiting a friend's house and they notice a cut on your arm and in response to recognizing your injury they offer you medical attention, as they wash and dress the wound how do you respond? If you are like most, and you were raised by parents who taught you to be respectful to others your response is likely to be to thank them for the specific act of tending to your wound and then complement them on their character or the characteristic that was revealed by their actions. You are likely to say thank you for bandaging my arm, you are very thoughtful or you are so kind. In this example, the first statement thank you for bandaging my arm is an expression of thanksgiving and the second you are so thoughtful or you are so kind is an expression of praise. Thanksgiving expresses appreciation for the specific act or action taken and praise is an acknowledgement of the person's nature. When I think of the difference between thanksgiving and praise I think of how little children react to the people around them. Children especially young children no not have the conceptual ability to distinguish between a given act or action and the underlying character trait that causes the action to occur and as a result children often judge whether a person is good or bad based solely upon how the child perceives or feels about a given action taken. Therefore, if you give a child who is not mature enough to distinguish between an action and the character that results in the action and the child does not like what is done to them, then the child's opinion of what happen will be transferred to the person who did it to the Child. Therefore, the Child only sees the person favorably when the child enjoys what was done. This is how many in the Body of Christ see God. God is good as long as He is doing what they expect or desire. However the question is can we acknowledge that God is good when we do not like what we are experiencing in our walk with Him. In the 5th verse of the 100th division of psalms the psalmist declared "The Lord is good" but God is not good because He does good things or things we think are good, God is good because that is His nature, in fact everything God does is good because God is good. One of the greatest challenges of a Christian is maintaining a posture of praise towards God in the midst of trying times. In those times when death, sickness, financial loss occur we may not recognize much we have to be thankful for but we should still be able to maintain a posture of praise towards God because God is good even in difficult times, because God is worthy of praise because of who He is, and not because of what He does. I do not believe any character in the Bible demonstrates the ability to praise God in the midst of adversity better that Job. In the 1st through 22nd verses of the first Chapter of the Book of Job the Bible states "There was a man in the land of Uz, whose name was Job; and that man was perfect and upright, and one that feared God, and eschewed evil. And there were born unto him seven sons and three daughters. His substance also was seven thousand sheep, and three thousand camels, and five hundred yoke of oxen, and five hundred she asses, and a very great household; so that this man was the greatest of all the men of the east. And his sons went and feasted in their houses, every one his day; and sent and called for their three sisters to eat and to drink with them. And it was so, when the days of their feasting were gone about, that Job sent and sanctified them, and rose up early in the morning, and offered burnt offerings according to the number of them all: for Job said, It may be that my sons have sinned, and cursed God in their hearts. Thus did Job continually. Now there was a day when the sons of God came to present themselves before the Lord, and Satan came also among them. And the Lord said unto Satan, Whence comest thou? Then Satan answered the Lord, and said, From going to and fro in the earth, and from walking up and down in it. And the Lord said unto Satan, Hast thou considered my servant Job, that there is none like him in the earth, a perfect and an upright man, one that feareth God, and escheweth evil? Then Satan answered the Lord, and said, Doth Job fear God for nought? Hast not thou made a hedge about him, and about his house, and about all that he hath on every side? thou hast blessed the work of his hands, and his substance is increased in the land. But put forth thine hand now, and touch all that he hath, and he will curse thee to thy face. And the Lord said unto Satan, Behold, all that he hath is in thy power; only upon himself put not forth thine hand. So Satan went forth from the presence of the Lord. And there was a day when his sons and his daughters were eating and drinking wine in their eldest brother's house: And there came a messenger unto Job, and said, The oxen were plowing, and the asses feeding beside them: And the Sabeans fell upon them, and took them away; yea, they have slain the servants with the edge of the sword; and I only am escaped alone to tell thee. While he was yet speaking, there came also another, and said, The fire of God is fallen from heaven, and hath burned up the sheep, and the servants, and consumed them; and I only am escaped alone to tell thee. While he was yet speaking, there came also another, and said, The Chaldeans made out three bands, and fell upon the camels, and have carried them away, yea, and slain the servants with the edge of the sword; and I only am escaped alone to tell thee. While he was yet speaking, there came also another, and said, Thy sons and thy daughters were eating and drinking wine in their eldest brother's house: And, behold, there came a great wind from the wilderness, and smote the four corners of the house, and it fell upon the young men, and they are dead; and I only am escaped alone to tell thee. Then Job arose, and rent his mantle, and shaved his head, and fell down upon the ground, and worshipped, And said, Naked came I out of my mother's womb, and naked shall I return thither: the Lord gave, and the Lord hath taken away; blessed be the name of the Lord. In all this Job sinned not, nor charged God foolishly." I cannot imagine what It must have been like to experience what Job experienced, to lose everything in a matter of hours. I realize that there are many in the Body of Christ who have or are suffering great loss and I would never want to do or say anything to appear to minimize what they may be going through but I simply cannot imagines what could be worse than what he experienced. There are a couple of things I want to point out about this story. In the 9th through 11th verses of the first Chapter of the Book of

Job satan challenged whether Job truly praised God because of who God is or whether Job was merely thankful for what God does when the Bible declared "Satan answered the Lord, and said, Doth Job fear God for nought? Hast not thou made a hedge about him, and about his house, and about all that he hath on every side? thou hast blessed the work of his hands, and his substance is increased in the land. But put forth thine hand now, and touch all that he hath, and he will curse thee to thy face." In other words satan was implying that God had to pay for Job's praise. I realize that the concept of God having to pay us to praise Him seems, well, insane, after all He is God and we are His creation and it is only natural that we would praise Him. But I submit to you that while the idea of God having to purchase our praise is insane to me and to you, the idea of God having to purchase our praise is not so hard for many to believe. How many times have you witnessed or heard of Christians leaving the Church and walking away from God when tragedy strikes, the lose a job, a child, a spouse or some other thing in their life goes horribly wrong or how many people renounce their faith in God because of some experience occurred that was painful or distasteful, or perhaps a man or women of God is discovered to have committed a grave sin. What about those who have walked away from God because God failed to honor a request to heal a loved one. Is it really so difficult to believe that there are those who expect to be paid to praise God. How about you, is your praise of God contingent upon God granting you what you require? What is worse is that people are watching! Just imagine all of Job's friend's, his neighbors and even members of his family who watched Job make offerings to the Lord, perhaps heard Job talk about God's goodness. The younger men in his community that may have admired and looked up to Job, imagine all of the men and women who may have never have even met Job but heard of his wealth and his devotion to God, all of which were now watching to see what Job would do now. What will Job say now that everything is gone? How many people are watching you to see how you will respond in your times of trouble, they may be members of your church, your co-workers, your friends, even your children, There may even be people who have never even met you that are watching to see what you do when it does not appear that the God you serve is blessing you? How you or we respond in these difficult moments will not only reveal the truth of our faith but may determine whether others are drawn to Christ or turned away. When I think of the need to praise God because of who He is and not what he does I cannot help but think of the early church, many of whom were jailed, beaten and even killed but never stopped praising God. It is no wonder why the Church had so much power in those days. In the 16th through 25th verses of the 16th Chapter of the Book of Acts the Bible records one such occurrence and provides "And it came to pass, as we went to prayer, a certain damsel possessed with a spirit of divination met us, which brought her masters much gain by soothsaying: The same followed Paul and us, and cried, saying, These men are the servants of the most high God, which shew unto us the way of salvation. And this did she many days. But Paul, being grieved, turned and said to the spirit, I command thee in the name of Jesus Christ to come out of her. And he came out the same hour. And when her masters saw that the hope of their gains was gone, they caught Paul and Silas, and drew them into the marketplace unto the rulers, And brought them to the magistrates, saying, These men, being Jews, do exceedingly trouble our city, And teach customs, which are not lawful for us to receive, neither to observe, being Romans. And the multitude rose up together against them: and the magistrates rent off their clothes, and commanded to beat them. And when they had laid many stripes upon them, they cast them into prison, charging the jailor to keep them safely: Who, having received such a charge, thrust them into the inner prison, and made their feet fast in the stocks. And at midnight Paul and Silas prayed, and sang praises unto God: and the prisoners heard them." Can you imagine being arrested, beaten and imprisoned because you delivered someone who was possessed by an evil spirit, how you would feel, the heaviness of heart you would experience, the sense of abandonment you would feel. What is truly amazing is that in the midst of their suffering and mistreatment the Bible says that they prayed and sang praises to God. Paul and Silas understood the importance of praising God for who he is and not what He does. They like Job realized that they could not judge God's character based on what they were experiencing because while there will be moments when it looks like all is lost God is still good and worthy to be praised. Just think about the powerful testimony the other prisoners received as they watched Paul and Silas bruised, beaten and bloody praising God locked away in prison. Think about what they learned about Paul and Silas' commitment to God and how worthy of honor God must have been. When I read these passages of scripture I realize that in these scriptures Paul and Silas are facing the same test that we see in the 8th through 11th verses of the 1st Chapter of the Book of Job which reads "And the Lord said unto Satan, Hast thou considered my servant Job, that there is none like him in the earth, a perfect and an upright man, one that feareth God, and escheweth evil? Then Satan answered the Lord, and said, Doth Job fear God for nought? Hast not thou made a hedge about him, and about his house, and about all that he hath on every side? thou hast blessed the work of his hands, and his substance is increased in the land. But put forth thine hand now, and touch all that he hath, and he will curse thee to thy face." Have you ever faced this situation, if so, how did you respond, did you praise God because of His goodness even when things around you were falling apart or did your reaction demonstrate that you expect God to purchase your praise?

The next point I want to make is Job recognized God's goodness in spite of the circumstances he faced. I think that in order to truly understand the meaning or value of a statement we have to view the statement in terms of the context in which it was made because the failure to view a statement in its proper context often results in our missing the true importance of the statement. I think that this is especially true in the case of Job. In the 20th through 22nd verses of the 1st Chapter of the Book of Job the Bible declares "Then Job arose, and rent his mantle, and shaved his head, and fell down upon the ground, and worshipped, And said, Naked came I out of my mother's womb, and naked shall I return thither: the Lord gave, and the Lord hath taken away; blessed be the name of the Lord. In all this Job sinned not, nor charged God foolishly." Think about the situation that Job finds himself in at the time this statement is made. Job a man who is perfect in the eyes of God is living an ideal life. He has ten Children who honor and respect him and one another, he has material wealth, the respect of the community, devoted servants. In short Job is a man who has everything, in fact, Job's life is going so well that even satan gives God credit. Then suddenly tragedy literally comes out of no where. Isn't it funny how we can be riding a wave of success one day and find ourselves overwhelmed by grief and disaster the next. Well that is exactly what happen to Job, one day he was the picture of the man who has everything and the next everything was gone. Can you imagine how Job must have felt as tragic report after tragic report came in, as witness after witness after witness recount the events of that systematically destroyed the life that Job had known. Have you ever had a day when it seemed like everything fell apart, if you have then maybe you can understand how Job must have felt. To make matters worse, there was no single event that Job could point to that could explain what was happening. I cannot begin to imagine the magnitude of the sorrow that Job must have been feeling or the questions that must have ran through his mind. At the end of all of this Job is left alone to deal with all that he had experienced with out the benefit of even a single consoling word, not even form God. If we have any empathy at all we will recognize the magnitude of despair that Job must have experienced as the gravity of his loss settles in his mind, I would imagine that Job's first response was shock, then denial, then the overwhelming sense of loss. The Bible tell us about Job's state of mind in the 20th verse of the 1st Chapter of Job when it says "Then job arose, and rent his mantle, and shaved his head" In our culture these actions do not really mean much but in the culture in which Job lived they were powerful indications of Job's grief and despair. The act of renting or tearing ones clothing was perhaps the most dramatic expression of grief a man could perform, and for a man to shave his head was a sign of shame and dishonor. However in the midst of Job's expression of shame and grief the Bible declares that Job "fell down upon the ground, and worshipped" Job did not ask God why, he did not run from God, He did not petition God to return what was lost, he did not complain about what had occurred, he did not do what many in the modern Church would do if they were faced with such a staggering series of events, he worshipped God. This should be a lesson to all of us that despite what is going on in our lives God is worthy of our worship. In the 21st verse of the 1st Chapter of the Book of Job the Bible provides that Job responded by saying "and, said naked came I out of my mothers womb, and naked shall I return thither: the Lord gave, and the Lord hath taken away; blessed be the name of the Lord." This is such a powerful statement and such an amazing expression of praise. Job was not in denial about his condition, he was not pretending that the events of the day had not transpired, Job just expressed his recognition that God was worthy to be praised despite of what he was going through, that God deserved to be praised because God is good not because of what God does. Could this be why the Bible describes Job as perfect and upright, because Job recognized that God was good even when Job's circumstances were not? What about you, do you praise God even when things in your life are not going well or do you only praise God when times are good? In the 14th through 18th verses of the Book of Daniel we see another example of men who praised God in the midst of difficult circumstances which provides "Nebuchadnezzar spake and said unto them, Is it true, O Shadrach, Meshach, and Abednego, do not ye serve my gods, nor worship the golden image which I have set up? Now if ye be ready that at what time ye hear the sound of the cornet, flute, harp, sackbut, psaltery, and dulcimer, and all kinds of musick, ye fall down and worship the image which I have made; well: but if ye worship not, ye shall be cast the same hour into the midst of a burning fiery furnace; and who is that God that shall deliver you out of my hands? Shadrach, Meshach, and Abednego, answered and said to the king, O Nebuchadnezzar, we are not careful to answer thee in this matter. If it be so, our God whom we serve is able to deliver us from the burning fiery furnace, and he will deliver us out of thine hand, O king. But if not, be it known unto thee, O king, that we will not serve thy gods, nor worship the golden image which thou hast set up" what a statement! Can you imagine finding yourself in a situation where you are forced to choose between giving the praise and worship that is due only to God to a false god created by man or face destruction? Would it surprise you to know that we find ourselves in this situation almost everyday, that we are given a choice to praise the gods of money, sex, security, success, ambition and a host of the gods of this world everyday, many of us do not realize it but everyday Christians all around the world bow down to these false gods and in so doing say that God is not able, not able to protect them, provide for them, comfort them, or even lead them, unlike shadrach, Meshach, and Abednego. As I think about the story of these young men and their response to Nebuchadnezzar I cannot help but ask how do we respond to pressure. The most basic reading of the third chapter of the book of Daniel makes it clear that these young men were not in a position of power and by all appearances their lives were in the hands of the king. It should be clear that disobeying the king could have dire consequences. It is also clear that the only protection they could have hoped to find from the king's judgment was from God. There are no courts to appeal to, no congress that can pass a law to protect them, no embassies where they can seek asylum, and no means of escape. Have you ever been in a situation where you could not see a way out, where there were no acceptable options? Well if you think your situation was touchy try trading places with these guys. Try standing before a king who demands that you choose between worshipping his god and living or worshipping your God and facing an unimaginably horrible death. What is worse yet your God is silent, no words of assurance, no burning bush, no sign of His intentions to save you, not even a strong gush of wind that might put out the fire, Hardly a situation that would inspire you to praise God is it? These are the moments where our choices matter, everyone will praise God after a victory but what will we do when the outcome seems uncertain or what is worse when it appears that all hope is lost. These are the moments when our maturity is measured, the moments when why we praise God becomes clear. Because if we can only praise God when His blessings or protection is clear we run the risk of failing God when it matters most, when we cannot see Him or His plan. But isn't that the real test of our faith, whether we believe God is good, God is faithful, God is able even, no especially, when we see no evidence He will. Isn't this what the Apostle Paul spoke of in the 1st verse of the 11th Chapter of the Book of Hebrews when he wrote "Now faith is the substance of things hoped for, the evidence of things not seen" Isn't that the basis of true praise, the ability to acknowledge God's goodness, His power, His love, His protection, His generosity when the evidence of these things is unseen. Isn't that exactly what Job did in the 21st verse of the 1st Chapter of the Book of Job when he said " The Lord gave and the Lord hath taken away; blessed be the name of the Lord." And isn't that what Shadrach, Meshach and Abednego did in the 17th and 18th verses of the 3rd Chapter of the Book of Daniel when they declared "If it be so, our God whom we serve is able to deliver us from the burning fiery furnace, and he will deliver us out of thine hand, O king. But if not, be it known unto thee, O king, that we will not serve thy gods, nor worship the golden image which thou hast set up" that I will praise God even when my circumstance are not what I want or need them to be. What would it say about our love for God if we were only willing to praise Him when He honored our requests or obeyed our commands could we really even call that love? How about you, can you imagine your spouse, your children only telling you they love and appreciate you when you are giving them what they desire, would you call that love, would that please you? I think the fact many can only manage to talk about God's goodness, His kindness, His mercy or any of the thousand upon thousands of God's attributes when they can see God's hand working in their life in a way that pleases them speaks volumes about the state of the Body of Christ and the increasing carnality in the Church as well as our loss of distinctiveness in the larger society. If we are going to become the light on the world that our Lord Jesus spoke of in 14th and 15th verses of the 5th Chapter of the Gospel according to Saint Matthew we are going to have to begin to examine our values and our commitment to living the life that Christ intended as oppose to living a life so define by material possession and convenience that we define God more as our provider that we do the true object of our praise. Further in order truly examine whether our values are truly what God requires we are going to have to seriously consider the admonishment of the Apostle Paul in the 1st and 2nd verses of the 12 Chapter of the Romans which provides "I beseech you therefore, brethren, by the mercies of God that you present your bodies a living sacrifice, Holy, acceptance unto God, which is your reasonable service. And be not conformed to this world: but be ye transformed by the renewing of your mind, that ye may prove what is that good, and acceptable, and perfect will of God." Or as the Amplified translation provides " I appeal to you therefore, brethren, and beg of you in view of [all] the mercies of God, to make a decisive dedication of your bodies-presenting all your members and facilities- as a living sacrifice, holy (devoted, consecrated) and well pleasing to God, which is your reasonable (rational, intelligent) service and spiritual worship. Do not be conformed to this world- the age, fashioned after and adopted to its external, superficial customs. But be transformed (changed) by the [entire] renewal of your mind-by its new ideals and its new attitude-so that you may prove [for yourselves] what is the good and acceptable and perfect will of God [in his sight for you]." But if we are not to be conform to image of this world but be transformed by the renewing of our minds shouldn't we think differently, react differently that the world, shouldn't our desires and aspirations be different, should we place a greater value on having a relationship with God, than we do on having the things of this world? I realize that if most members of the Body of Christ were to answer these questions they would answer that they do, but if that is true would we, the Body of Christ, think the way we do pray the way we do, praise the way we do? Wouldn't there be more of an emphasis on what we have in Him and less on what we want in the world? Wouldn't our attitude be more like the attitude expressed by Job in the 21st verse of the 1st Chapter of the Book of Job when he said "naked came I out of my mother's womb, and naked shall I return thither: The Lord gave and the Lord hath taken away; blessed be the name of the Lord." Wouldn't we give God the type of praise that gives God's glory?

The next point that I want to address is that praising God for who He is and not simply what He does gives God glory. It should be well understood by now that our lives were intended to glorify God. In fact this truth is clearly established in the 7th verse of the 43rd Chapter of the Book of Isaiah which provides "Even every one that is called by my name: for I have created him for my glory, I have formed him; yea, I have made him." To glorify God is to give God weight, significance or honor, to place a greater value on God in comparison to everything else. When we praise God in spite of our circumstances we communicate to God and to the world that God is more significant to us than what we may believe we lack. On the other hand, when we are unwilling to offer God praise when things are not working in our favor, we are denying God the glory due Him and glorifying the things we desire. Furthermore, satan's goal is to cause us to deny God glory and to cause us instead to glorify the things of this word. In the 9th through 11th verses of the 1st Chapter of the Book of Job the Bible records satan's response to God's suggestion that satan consider Job and provides "Then satan answered the Lord, and said Doth Job fear God for nought? Hast not thou made a hedge about him, and about his house, and about all that he hath on every side? Thou hast blessed the works of his hands, and his substance is increased in the land. But put forth thine hand now, and touch all that he hath, and he will curse thee to thy face" satan's response challenges the very nature of Job's relationship with God and our as well. At the heart of satan's statement lies a question that the entire world is waiting to have answered, do they truly love and reverence God or are they simply using God to get what they want and need from Him. The question that I believe is at the heart of satan's statement is first and foremost a question of motive. Do we praise God because we think He is worthy or because we hope He is willing to do for us what we cannot do for ourselves, in other words if you knew that God would refuse to grant another request or respond to another prayer, would you still praise Him? Satan is betting that you won't but I am praying that you would. Just imagine the joy satan would have gotten, the pleasure he would have experienced if job, like some in the Body of Christ have, cursed God because of what he had suffered. What would it have said about the value that Job places on his relationship with God if he refused to praise God because he suffered the loss of the things he possessed in the world? How could he ever again say that he loved or honored God if he abandoned God because he experienced adversity, for that matter how could we?

Life in this world is filled with difficult times and painful events however the one thing that always remains constant is that God will always be with us. Through the most painful and devastating times we have the assurance that the God who knows all, sees all, and can heal all is there for us always watching over us. The question is, is that enough to cause us to praise Him or are we justified in asking for more in exchange for our praise? The answer to this question depends on how we see God do we see God as Holy, sovereign, beautiful, righteous, loving or do we see God simply as a supplier. At the core of satan's response to God in the 9th through 11th verses of the 1st Chapter of the Book of Job is the belief that we, who say that we love God above all else are lying and that when tested the truth of what is really in our hearts will be revealed, that we value the creation more than the creator and simply put we value the things of this world more than we loved God. The question is, is he right, do we love our homes, careers, our families, our money, or even our lives more than we love God? In the 24th verse of the 6th Chapter of the Gospel according to the Saint Matthew Jesus warned us about our attachment to the things of this world when He declared "No man can serve two masters: for either he will hate the one, and love the other; or else he will hold to the one, and despise the other. Ye cannot serve God and Mammon" and isn't this really the problem with our praising God simply for who He is, our love and attachment to the things of this world? If we had the attitude of Job, the Lord gave and the Lord hath taken it away, would our praise then be about Him? As I think about the question of our praise I am reminded of the admonishment given to the Church by the Apostle John in the 15th and 16th verses of the 2nd Chapter of the 1st Epistle of John when He wrote "Love not the world, neither the things that are in the World. If any man loves the world, the love for the Father is not in him. For all that is in the world, the lust of the flesh, and the lust of the eyes, and the pride of life, is not of the Father, but is of the world" however, for many in the Body of Christ our love for the world is greater than our love for the father, or for Christ. The problem that we face is that we come from the world and in far too many instances have been shaped and defined by it. What makes this problem worse is that far too few have given far too little thought about how contrary our motives and desires are to the plan and purposes of the God we profess to love or the Lord we profess to serve. Far too often we are so consumed with our pursuit of the things of this world that we cannot hear God challenging us to change our values, priorities and ideals. Far too often we are so focused on God's mercy that we lose sight of His desire that we grow and mature. One of the greatest indications of our spiritual maturity is how we see God, as spiritual children, much like natural children, we see our father our God in the limited sense of what He does or does not do for us without the ability or perhaps even without the willingness to come to know Him, value Him and praise Him for who He is.

9.

ELEMENT NINE

The Believers understanding that God deserves more than He asks for.

It is only fitting that this would be the last chapter of this work because as believers this is the greatest truth of our lives. God deserves more than He asks for! In each of the proceeding chapters we have discussed an element of the relationship that God desires to have with each of us and I realize that those elements may appear to require a lot but in actuality they are nothing compared to what God truly deserves. I believe that as Christians one of our greatest challenges is not to get so caught up in what we need from God that we forget about God. Yes God is our provider, our healer, our sustainer, and our protector but God is so much more than what we need from Him or what he does for us and if that is all we see we will never come to see much less appreciate God. In the 1st through 9th verses of the 8th division of psalms David writes "O LORD our Lord, how excellent is thy name in all the earth! who hast set thy glory above the heavens. Out of the mouth of babes and sucklings hast thou ordained strength because of thine enemies, that thou mightest still the enemy and the avenger. When I consider thy heavens, the work of thy fingers, the moon and the stars, which thou hast ordained; what is man, that thou art mindful of him? and the son of man, that thou visitest him? For thou hast made him a little lower than the angels, and hast crowned him with glory and honor. Thou madest him to have dominion over the works of thy hands; thou hast put all things under his feet: all sheep and oxen, yea, and the beasts of the field; the fowl of the air, and the fish of the sea, and whatsoever passeth through the paths of the seas. O LORD our Lord, how excellent is thy name in all the earth!" In this scripture David begins to express his amazement at the wonder of God's creation and the message it conveys about God. Have you ever stopped to consider God's creation in all of its beauty and complexity and then imagine the mind and the heart that would or could create such wonder or the generosity of a God that would provide us with so much and request so little in return, for what does God actually ask for but that we love Him and that we love one another because we are made in His image. It should be evident that all God ever asks for is a portion of what He has already given us, because God is the creator of all things there is nothing we have that is not a gift to us from God. Every command from God relating to our giving whether it is a tithe or an offering, or even the Sabbath is based on God's desire that we give to Him a portion of what He has so graciously given to us. In the 8th through 11th verses of the 20th Chapter of the Book of Exodus Moses expressing God's instructions concerning the Sabbath declared "Remember the Sabbath day, to keep it holy. Six days shalt thou labor, and do all thy work: but the seventh day is the Sabbath of the LORD thy God: in it thou shalt not do any work, thou, nor thy son, nor thy daughter, thy manservant, nor thy maidservant, nor thy cattle, nor thy stranger that is within thy gates: for in six days the LORD made heaven and earth, the sea, and all that in them, and rested the seventh day: wherefore the LORD blessed the Sabbath day, and hallowed it." By establishing the Sabbath God required that the Nation of Israel reserve the seventh day for God. During that day, which was traditionally observed from sun down on Friday until sun down on Saturday, (based on the lunar calendar), the Nation of Israel was required to cease or rest from all work and instead worship God. When I consider the requirement of the Sabbath I find it interesting that God who created time and the hours and days that define it, only asked that 24 of the 168 hours of the week be devoted to Him with the remaining 144 hours to be uses at their discretion. Just try to imagine that for a moment, God in an act of pure love and generosity creates the earth and all of it splendor, the trees that produce our food, the water that we drink, the beauty of the mountains, the vastness of the plains, the depths of the valleys and every living thing on the earth, creates time and gives us the right to occupy and rule over it and all He asks in return is that we give Him a small portion of what He has so graciously gives us. 24 hours out of every 168 and in fact it is actually only 16 hours that He reserves because for most of us 8 of the 24 hours that we are to devote to Him are actually spent sleeping. I wonder how many of us ever stop to think about how little God really asks of us. The tragic thing is how few of us even bother to comply with such a small demand and quite frankly view it as unreasonable. I realize that most members of the Body of Christ would argue that we no longer worship God on the Sabbath but rather our day of worship is now on Sunday, but does changing the day make our response any better? Do we honestly believe that the two or three hours we give God on Sunday morning satisfies God's requirement simply because we choose to change the day we choose to reserve for Him, are we suggesting that the two or three hours we offer Him is equal to the 24 hours He requires because of the day of the week we have decided to give Him. Or are we actually suggesting as some might that because God was gracious enough to send His only begotten Son to die for our sins, that God is now deserving of less time? Has God's sovereignty diminished because He has provided us with the gift of salvation, is he less deserving, is His guidance, fellowship, approval less important than it was when we were bound by the law? In the alternative should the receipt of such an amazing gift result in our giving God more and not less? According to the Apostle Paul the answer is clearly yes. In the 1st through 11th verses of the 4th Chapter of the Book of Hebrews the Apostle Paul wrote "Let us therefore fear, lest, a promise being left us of entering into his rest, any of you should seem to come short of it. For unto us was the gospel preached, as well as unto them: but the word preached did not profit them, not being mixed with faith in them that heard it. For we which have believed do enter into rest, as he said, As I have sworn in my wrath, if they shall enter into my rest: although the works were finished from the foundation of the world. For he spake in a certain place of the seventh day on this wise, And God did rest the seventh day from all his works. And in this place again, if they shall enter into my rest. Seeing therefore it remaineth that some must enter therein, and they to whom it was first preached entered not in because of unbelief: again, he limiteth a certain day, saying in David, Today, after so long a time; as it is said, Today if ye will hear his voice, harden not your hearts. For if Jesus had given them rest, then would he not afterward have spoken of another day. There remaineth therefore a rest to the people of God. For he that is entered into his rest, he also hath ceased from his own works, as God did from his. Let us labor therefore to enter into that rest, lest any man fall after the same example of unbelief." In writing these passages the Apostle Paul articulates a new understanding of the Sabbath spoken of in the 8th through 11th verses of the 20th Chapter of the Book of Exodus, one that transcends visitation into habitation, one that changes the Sabbath from a day to be set aside to a life to be lived. However, even this new standard is far less than what God actually deserves. Once again what God demands relating to the Sabbath rest spoken of by the Apostle Paul is but a small portion of what God has given us. This Sabbath which is in its most basic form represents a surrender of our hearts and our priorities is a small price to pay for the life that Jesus surrendered for us on the cross. Jesus surrendered His will to the father, for our sakes, even to the point of death. In the 14th through 17th verses of the 5th Chapter of the 2nd Book of Corinthians the apostle Paul speaking on the new Sabbath wrote "For the love of Christ constraineth us; because we thus judge, that if one died for all, then were all dead: and that he died for all, that they which live should not henceforth live unto themselves, but unto him which died for them, and rose again. Wherefore henceforth know we no man after the flesh: yea, though we have known Christ after the flesh, yet now henceforth know we him no more. Therefore if any man be in Christ, he is a new creature: old things are passed away; behold, all things are become new." These passages of scripture established the basis for the Sabbath rest in the 4th Chapter of the Book of Hebrews, Christ died for all therefore we are all to live for Him. When I think of the reality of Christ's death for me and the corresponding commandment that I live for Him it becomes clear that God, who had the right to demand that I die for my own sins, but instead requires only that I live for Him, deserves much more than He asks for and much more that I could have ever paid. This point becomes ever clearer in light of the Apostle Paul's writing in the 1st and 2nd verses of the 12th Chapter of the Book of Romans where he writes " I beseech you therefore, brethren, by the mercies of God, that ye present your bodies a living sacrifice, holy, acceptable unto God, which is your reasonable service. And be not conformed to this world: but be ye transformed by the renewing of your mind, that ye may prove what is that good, and acceptable, and perfect will of God." Or as the amplified translation provides "I appeal to you therefore, brethren, and beg of you in view of [all] the mercies of God, to make a decisive dedication of your bodies [presenting all your members and faculties] as a living sacrifice, holy (devoted, consecrated) and well pleasing to God, which is your reasonable (rational, intelligent) service and spiritual worship. Do not be conformed to this world (this age), [fashioned after and adapted to its external, superficial customs], but be transformed (changed) by the [entire] renewal of your mind [by its new ideals and its new attitude], so that you may prove [for yourselves] what is the good and acceptable and perfect will of God, even the thing which is good and acceptable and perfect [in His sight for you]." For some in the Body of Christ the reality of not conforming to the image of the world, its ideals, it definitions of success, its focus on material possessions in exchange for what may, at least at first, appear to be a boring and drab life might seem like an unreasonable or at least an unnatural request but is it really? I suppose if we were to look at what God requires of us in a vacuum it might appear that way, but is it really so great of a demand that God who sent His son to die for us to ask us to live for Him? Is the sacrifice of our social life a lot compared to Christ's sacrifice of His literal life? For that matter, should we even be asking this question since the life we would be giving up is not ours anyway? Is it unreasonable for the creator to do what He desires with His creation? The plain truth is that God has always had the right to do with our lives as He chooses because they have always belonged to

Him. God had and has every right to demand that each one of us bare the full consequences of our sin and disobedience, to require each of us to die on our own cross for payment or even worse to spend eternity in hell for our sins. But God because of His goodness, His kindness, His compassionate love towards us, does not demand what He deserves, He does not ask for what we owe, He asks for only a small portion, God through out the Bible has never asked for what He deserves but instead asks for a portion. Not only has God given us redemption through Jesus Christ, but God has given us dominion over all of creation. In the 26th through 29th verses of the 1st Chapter of the Book of Genesis the Bible provides "And God said, Let us make man in our image, after our likeness: and let them have dominion over the fish of the sea, and over the fowl of the air, and over the cattle, and over all the earth, and over every creeping thing that creepeth upon the earth. So

God created man in his own image, in the image of God created he him; male and female created he them. And God blessed them, and God said unto them, Be fruitful, and multiply, and replenish the earth, and subdue it: and have dominion over the fish of the sea, and over the fowl of the air, and over every living thing that moveth upon the earth. And God said, Behold, I have given you every herb bearing seed, which is upon the face of all the earth, and every tree, in the which is the fruit of a tree yielding seed; to you it shall be for meat." I wonder how many in the Body of Christ have ever taken time to consider these verses of scripture, how many of us ever consider the beauty or the magnitude of God's gifts to us. In the society in which we live, especially those of us in the western world, with all the hustle and bustle, the pressure to succeed, to achieve, it is easy to get so consumed with what we are trying to accomplish for ourselves that it becomes difficult to find time to really think about what God has done for us. Everything that there is exists because of God, There is so much we take for granted. When was the last time you considered the impact of air or water on civilization or on your life? How often do we remind ourselves that if it was not for a specific act of God, there would be no air to breath or water to drink? As I have followed the exploration of space I have gained more and more appreciation for the act of creation reveal to us in the 1st Chapter of the book of Genesis. Man has discovered millions if not billions of planets in space but earth is the only planet with liquid water, or an atmosphere that could sustain life as we know it, just take a moment to grasp that concept. Earth is the only planet that God made that could sustain life. As I begin to learn more and more about space I began to realize just how unique and how extraordinary the earth really is, not only because of its atmosphere, but also in terms of its size and weight, the speed at which it rotates around the sun, the angle at which it tilts, its temperature, it proximity to the sun. However, you do not have to explore space to see how amazing God's act of creation is. If we were to study the oceans we would discover the amazing diversity of life that lives under them some just under the surface of the waters, others close to the ocean floor, each one serving a specific purpose. All of which were designed by God for His glory and our benefit. Then there are the birds that fly through the air which are almost as diverse as the life that live in the oceans, birds as small as a humming bird and as large as an eagle, Birds like the ostrich that do not even fly, creatures that can see at great distances during the day, birds that see better at night and even bats that cannot see at all. All of which are part of the splendor of God's creation. When was the last time you took time to consider the grandeur of it all, the power of a volcano, the strength of the wind, the force of a raging river all of which are a testament to the greatness of God, all of which create a majestic portrait of His brilliance and His glory. All of this and so much more was created by God and handed over to us simply because he loves us and desires to bless us. Even though He knew that we would betray Him He still created us and desires to bless us. Throughout the History of man, God has consistently demonstrated His love for us and His desire to have a relationship with us and asks very little in return. I remember when I as a teenager and I was first taught the ten commandments and was told that there were things that we forbidden for me to do by God and other things that God required of me how disappointed I was in the knowledge that there were requirements that came along with my relationship with God I professed to desire. I thought that God should permit or at least tolerate any behavior that I believed to be necessary, natural or desirable at any given time and when I discovered that I was wrong, I was devastated. I thought how could a God who professed to love me, tell me that there were things that He required of me, I thought that it was unfair! The problem was I had heard of God, believed in God but had never met God, the problem was that spiritually I was immature and had no understanding of who God was, no understanding of God's sovereignty, no understanding that God was all knowing or all powerful, and what is worse I had no real understanding of what I was saved from and still needed to be saved (delivered) from and no real understanding of either the real price of my salvation (paid by Jesus) or the promises that God had made the world about my life. I had neither come to know or love God, the good new was that while I had not yet come to know God, God knew me and while I had not yet come to love God, God loved me. As I listen to what is spoken by the members of the Body of Christ, the culture of willfulness, and self rule that seems to dominate the conversation, the all but complete abandonment of God's clear instructions concerning life in Christ I wonder how many in the Body of Christ, even those in leadership positions are stuck where I was when I first came to Christ, so focused on what they desired that they are blind to what God deserves. I believe that one of the greatest challenges we as believers face is the challenge of true Christian maturity, the process of becoming and the practice of living as spiritual adults, Further, I believe that our ability to come to understand the staggeringly great gifts we have been given and how little we have been ask to give in return is a significant part of that process. Whenever, I think about how little that is required of us compared to how much God truly deserves I cannot help but think about the day over two thousand years ago when Jesus stood trial and was sentenced to death for the crimes we committed against God. In the 2nd through 47th the verse of the 23rd Chapter of the Gospel according to Saint Luke The Bible contains the story of Jesus' payment for our sins and provides "And they began to accuse him, saying, We found this fellow perverting the nation, and forbidding to give tribute to Cæsar, saying that he himself is Christ a King. And Pilate asked him, saying, Art thou the King of the Jews? And he answered him and said, Thou sayest it. Then said Pilate to the chief priests and to the people, I find no fault in this man. And they were the more fierce, saying, He stirreth up the people, teaching throughout all Jewry, beginning from Galilee to this place. When Pilate heard of Galilee, he asked whether the man were a Galileans. And as soon as he knew that he belonged unto Herod's jurisdiction, he sent him to Herod, who himself also was at Jerusalem at that time. And when Herod saw Jesus, he was exceeding glad: for he was desirous to see him of a long season, because he had heard many things of him; and he hoped to have seen some miracle done by him. Then he questioned with him in many words; but he answered him nothing. And the chief priests and scribes stood and vehemently accused him. And Herod with his men of war set him at nought, and mocked him, and arrayed him in a gorgeous robe, and sent him again to Pilate. And the same day Pilate and Herod were made friends together: for before they were at enmity between themselves. And Pilate, when he had called together the chief priests and the rulers and the people, said unto them, Ye have brought this man unto me, as one that perverteth the people: and, behold, I, having examined him before you, have found no fault in this man touching those things whereof ye accuse him: no, nor yet Herod: for I sent you to him; and, lo, nothing worthy of death is done unto him. I will therefore chastise him, and release him. (For of necessity he must release one unto them at the feast.) And they cried out all at once, saying, Away with this man, and release unto us Barabbas: (who for a certain sedition made in the city, and for murder, was cast into prison.) Pilate therefore, willing to release Jesus, spake again to them. But they cried, saying, crucify him, crucify him. And he said unto them the third time, Why, what evil hath he done? I have found no cause of death in him: I will therefore chastise him, and let him go. And they were instant with loud voices, requiring that he might be crucified. And the voices of them and of the chief priests prevailed. And Pilate gave sentence that it should be as they required. And he released unto them him that for sedition and murder was cast into prison, whom they had desired; but he delivered Jesus to their will. And as they led him away, they laid hold upon one Simon, a Cyrenian, coming out of the country, and on him they laid the cross, that he might bear it after Jesus. And there followed him a great company of people, and of women, which also bewailed and lamented him. But Jesus turning unto them said, Daughters of Jerusalem, weep not for me, but weep for yourselves, and for your children. For, behold, the days are coming, in the which they shall say, Blessed are the barren, and the wombs that never bare, and the paps which never gave suck. Then shall they begin to say to the mountains, Fall on us; and to the hills, Cover us. For if they do these things in a green tree, what shall be done in the dry? And there were also two other, malefactors, led with him to be put to death. And when they were come to the place, which is called Calvary, there they crucified him, and the malefactors, one on the right hand, and the other on the left. Then said Jesus, Father, forgive them; for they know not what they do. And they parted his raiment, and cast lots. And the people stood beholding. And the rulers also with them derided him, saying, He saved others; let him save himself, if he be Christ, the chosen of God. And the soldiers also mocked him, coming to him, and offering him vinegar, and saying, If thou be the king of the Jews, save thyself. And a superscription also was written over him in letters of Greek, and Latin, and Hebrew, THIS IS THE KING OF THE JEWS. And one of the malefactors which were hanged railed on him, saying, If thou be Christ, save thyself and us. But the other answering rebuked him, saying, Dost not thou fear God, seeing thou art in the same condemnation? And we indeed justly; for we receive the due reward of our deeds: but this man hath done nothing amiss. And he said unto Jesus, Lord, remember me when thou comest into thy kingdom. And Jesus said unto him, Verily I say unto thee, To day shalt thou be with me in paradise. And it was about the sixth hour, and there was a darkness over all the earth until the ninth hour. And the sun was darkened, and the veil of the temple was rent in the midst. And when Jesus had cried with a loud voice, he said, Father, into thy hands I commend my spirit: and having said thus, he gave up the ghost. Now when the centurion saw what was done, he glorified God, saying, Certainly this was a righteous man" What could God ever ask of us that could come close to being equal to the price Jesus paid for us on the Cross or for the blessings that our faith in Him make available to us? What could God ask for from us or require from us that is equal to the complete restoration of our position as children of God or our redemption back into our role of God's stewards', God's ambassadors on the earth? Is there any amount of money that is worth more that what God has given us, can we give God what is already His in exchange for what He has given us? Do our words, our expressions of gratitude, out acts of service, our promises of worship come close to repaying God for what He has given us, the questions hardly seems worth answering, but the answer is clearly NO. There is nothing more valuable that our salvation through Christ Jesus and the promise of restoration and redemption that it brings. But the good news is God does not ask for what He deserves, our salvation is a gift freely given and all God truly asks of us is that we believe, believe that Jesus is out Lord, believe that through Him we have the victory, believe that His word is true. This is all God asked for but it is far less than God deserves. But our ability to understand this truth, truly is an element of our maturity that I pray we all come to.

CONCLUSION

Each of us were endowed by God with a desire for something more, something that most of us cannot place our finger on. This desire drives some to great heights of creation, others great discovery, and others still great destruction. It was intended to drive us to the greatest of all things God!! However in order for any of us to complete a journey to a destination, to a place that we have never been we will need to rely on both maps and tools. In the case of this Journey the only map you will ever truly need is the word of God but the tools that we will need to rely on are many. It is my prayer that this work will be deemed worthy to become one of yours. In writing this book it was my singular desire to provide information which I believe will prove helpful in provoking an examination of where we are and what we truly believe about our responses to both God, as well as what we demonstrate to those who may only see God through us. I believe that each of us must make a honest assessment of not only where we are in God but perhaps more importantly where we must grow in God. We are in what I believe to be a great cross roads in the History of the Body of Christ a point of divergence where we must choice for ourselves which way we should go and further must clearly understand the Choices we are making and the consequences they will produce. I hope that in some small what this way book will serve as a tool in that regard. I do not presume to have all the answers or to stand in a position to answer these questions for anyone other than myself, but I none the less hope that I can at least help you frame the question, and may help point the way to what I believe the answers to be. Finally, in the depth of my heart I believe that the greatest honor any person can have is to be called the child of their father and matured to a place where that Father not only loves but trust them as children. That is my desire for each of you that you mature to a place where our Father in heaven trust you as well as loves you. I pray that this book will serve as a tool for you in your efforts to mature to that place.

www.ingramcontent.com/pod-product-compliance
Lightning Source LLC
Chambersburg PA
CBHW072002150426
43194CB00008B/969